Microsoft® SharePoint® Designer 2007

Level 1

Microsoft® SharePoint® Designer 2007: Level 1

Part Number: 084721
Course Edition: 1.0

NOTICES

HELP US IMPROVE OUR COURSEWARE

Your comments are important to us. Please contact us at Element K Press LLC, 1-800-478-7788, 500 Canal View Boulevard, Rochester, NY 14623, Attention: Product Planning, or through our Web site at **http://support.elementkcourseware.com**.

Microsoft® SharePoint® Designer 2007: Level 1

About This Course

You've created intranet sites using Microsoft® Windows® SharePoint® Services. There will be times when you would want to build sites that lay emphasis on your company's unique requirements and sites that align themselves with the company's unique brand identity. In this course, you will use *Microsoft® SharePoint® Designer 2007* to customize your SharePoint sites and build a new subsite on the SharePoint services platform.

You would have created Windows SharePoint sites for your intranet, but ever wondered the lack of features to customize those sites? You might prefer a different color scheme or a different layout with different set of functionality or tailor your site to meet specific brand requirements. But such extensive customization tasks might prove to be cumbersome with WSS alone. *Microsoft® SharePoint® Designer 2007* is the answer to these requirements. With an easy to use WYSIWYG environment, SharePoint Designer helps you to leverage the SharePoint technologies and enables you to create and customize Microsoft SharePoint sites and build sophisticated application interfaces and workflows on the SharePoint platform, without the need to get into coding.

Course Description

Target Student

This course is intended for SharePoint web designers and SharePoint solution developers, who want to learn to customize SharePoint sites by enhancing the look and feel of a SharePoint site and also to create dynamic pages using Web Parts and workflows.

Course Prerequisites

Students should have taken the *Microsoft® Windows® SharePoint® Services 3.0: Level 1* course from Element K or have an equivalent knowledge.

Recommended, though not required, are the following courses:

- *Microsoft® Windows® SharePoint® Services 3.0: Level 2*
- Cascading Style Sheets (Third Edition)

How to Use This Book

As a Learning Guide

Each lesson covers one broad topic or set of related topics. Lessons are arranged in order of increasing proficiency with *Microsoft® SharePoint® Designer 2007*; skills you acquire in one lesson are used and developed in subsequent lessons. For this reason, you should work through the lessons in sequence.

We organized each lesson into results-oriented topics. Topics include all the relevant and supporting information you need to master *Microsoft® SharePoint® Designer 2007*, and activities allow you to apply this information to practical hands-on examples.

You get to try out each new skill on a specially prepared sample file. This saves you typing time and allows you to concentrate on the skill at hand. Through the use of sample files, hands-on activities, illustrations that give you feedback at crucial steps, and supporting background information, this book provides you with the foundation and structure to learn *Microsoft® SharePoint® Designer 2007* quickly and easily.

As a Review Tool

Any method of instruction is only as effective as the time and effort you are willing to invest in it. In addition, some of the information that you learn in class may not be important to you immediately, but it may become important later on. For this reason, we encourage you to spend some time reviewing the topics and activities after the course. For additional challenge when reviewing activities, try the "What You Do" column before looking at the "How You Do It" column.

As a Reference

The organization and layout of the book make it easy to use as a learning tool and as an after-class reference. You can use this book as a first source for definitions of terms, background information on given topics, and summaries of procedures.

Course Icons

Icon	Description
	A **Caution Note** makes students aware of potential negative consequences of an action, setting, or decision that are not easily known.
	Display Slide provides a prompt to the instructor to display a specific slide. Display Slides are included in the Instructor Guide only.
	An **Instructor Note** is a comment to the instructor regarding delivery, classroom strategy, classroom tools, exceptions, and other special considerations. Instructor Notes are included in the Instructor Guide only.
	Notes Page indicates a page that has been left intentionally blank for students to write on.
	A **Student Note** provides additional information, guidance, or hints about a topic or task.
	A **Version Note** indicates information necessary for a specific version of software.

Course Objectives

In this course, you will use Microsoft® SharePoint® Designer 2007 to create and modify a SharePoint site.

You will:

- familiarize yourself with the SharePoint Designer environment.
- create a new subsite.
- add content to a web page.
- use Cascading Style Sheets to format a SharePoint site.
- add basic functionality to web pages.
- add SharePoint components to the site.
- automate business processes with workflows.

Course Requirements

Hardware

You will need two servers for a class and one client computer for each person in the class, plus one computer for the instructor. For each of these machines, the following hardware requirements are the minimum suggested for this course:

- Pentium 4 2.0 GHz.
- 1 GB of RAM for the SharePoint Services 3.0 server, and 512 MB of RAM for all other machines.
- 4 GB of hard disk space.
- CD-ROM or DVD drive.
- VGA or higher video.
- Keyboard and mouse.
- A display system to project the instructor's computer screen.
- Internet access for all computers.

Software

The following software is required for the successful setup and completion of this course.

- Microsoft® Windows Server® 2003, Standard or Enterprise Edition
- Windows® Server 2003 Service Pack 2
- Microsoft® Windows XP Professional
- Windows XP Service Pack 2
- Microsoft® Windows® SharePoint Services® 3.0
- Microsoft® .NET Framework 3.0
- Microsoft® Office SharePoint® Designer 2007
- Microsoft® Office 2007 Professional or Professional Plus

Class Setup

The classroom environment consists of two Windows Servers: a domain controller/mail server and a SharePoint server, and one workstation for the instructor and one for each person in the class.

Create the Domain Controller/Mail Server

Complete the following steps to create the domain controller and mail server.

1. Install Microsoft Windows Server 2003, Standard or Enterprise Edition, with the following parameters:

Parameter	Value
Computer Name	DC
Administrator Password	!Pass1234

Parameter	Value
Workgroup Name	WORKGROUP

2. Install Windows Server 2003 Service Pack 2. When prompted, restart the computer and log on as Administrator.

3. Configure the network settings.

   a. Choose **Start→Control Panel→Network Connections→Local Area Connection.**

   b. Click **Properties,** select **Internet Protocol (TCP/IP),** and click **Properties.**

   c. Configure the network settings as follows:

      ■ **IP Address:** *192.168.1.200*

      ■ **Subnet Mask:** *255.255.255.0*

      ■ **Preferred DNS Server:** *192.168.1.200*

   d. Click **OK** twice, and then click **Close.**

4. Install the additional Windows components.

   a. Choose **Start→Control Panel→Add Or Remove Programs.**

   b. Click **Add/Remove Windows Components.**

   c. Verify that **Application Server** is checked, and check **Email Services.**

   d. Check the **Networking Services** check box and click **Details.**

   e. Check the **Domain Name System (DNS)** and **Windows Internet Name Service (WINS)** check boxes and click **OK.**

   f. Click **Next.**

   g. If prompted for the Windows 2003 disk, insert the disk and browse for the required files.

   h. When the installation is complete, click **Finish,** and then close the **Add Or Remove Programs** control panel.

5. Promote the server to a domain controller.

   a. Choose **Start→Command Prompt.**

   b. Type *dcpromo* and press **Enter.**

   c. Click **Next** twice.

   d. Verify that **Domain controller for a new domain** is selected and click **Next.**

   e. Verify that **Domain in a new forest** is selected and click **Next.**

   f. For **Domain Name,** type *ourglobalcompany.com* and click **Next.**

   g. For **Domain Default NetBIOS Name,** type *GLOBAL* and click **Next.**

   h. To accept the default database locations and **Shared System Volume,** click **Next** twice.

   i. Verify that **Install and configure the DNS server on this computer and set this computer to use this DNS server as its preferred DNS server** is selected, and click **Next.**

   j. Verify that **Permissions Compatible Only With Windows 2000 Or Windows Server 2003 Operating Systems** is selected, and click **Next.**

     k.   For the **Restore Mode Password,** enter and confirm *!Pass1234* and click **Next.**

     l.   Review the settings, and click **Next.**

     m.   Click **Finish** and click **Restart Now.**

     n.   When the computer restarts, log on as **Administrator.**

6.   Configure DNS.

     a.   Choose **Start→Administrative Tools→DNS.**

     b.   Expand **DC→Forward Lookup Zones→ourglobalcompany.com.**

     c.   Choose **Action→New Mail Exchanger.**

     d.   For **Fully Qualified Domain Name Of The Mail Server,** type *dc.ourglobalcompany.com* and click **OK.**

     e.   Choose **Action→New Alias (CNAME).**

     f.   For **Alias name (uses parent domain if left blank),** type *mail.*

     g.   For **Fully qualified domain name of the target host,** type *dc.ourglobalcompany.com* and click **OK.**

     h.   Close the DNS Management Console.

7.   Configure mail services.

     a.   Choose **Start→Administrative Tools→POP3 Service.**

     b.   Right-click **DC** and choose **Properties.**

     c.   Verify that **Authentication Method** is set to **Active Directory Integrated.**

     d.   Uncheck the **Always Create An Associated User For New Mailboxes** check box and click **OK.**

     e.   Select **DC** and click **New Domain.**

     f.   For **Domain Name,** type *ourglobalcompany.com* and click **OK.**

     g.   Expand **DC** and click **ourglobalcompany.com.**

     h.   Click **Add Mailbox,** type *administrator* and click **OK.**

     i.   If necessary, in the **POP3 Service** information box, check **Do not show this message again,** and click **OK.**

     j.   Close the POP3 Service Management Console.

8.   Create Active Directory user accounts. You can use several different tools to accomplish this including the **Active Directory Users And Computers Administrative Tool** and the `net user` command in a command prompt.

User's Display Name	Login Name	Password	Email Address
central	central	!Pass1234	central@ourglobalcompany.com
user01 through user12 (or as many as required)	user01 through user12 (or as many as required)	!Pass1234	user01@ourglobalcompany.com through user12@ourglobalcompany.com (or as many as required)
Susan Young	syoung	!Pass1234	syoung@ourglobalcompany.com

User's Display Name	Login Name	Password	Email Address
Bob Wheeler	bwheeler	!Pass1234	bwheeler@ourglobalcompany.com
Maria Miller	mmiller	!Pass1234	mmiller@ourglobalcompany.com

9. Create mailboxes for all users.

   a. Open the **POP3 Service** control panel.

   b. Expand **DC** and select **ourglobalcompany.com.**

   c. Click **Add Mailbox.**

   d. For **Mailbox Name,** type *central.*

   e. Click **OK.**

   f. If necessary, in the **POP3 Service** information box, check the **Do Not Show This Message Again** check box and click **OK.**

   g. Repeat steps 'c' to 'f' for all other user names that you added in the previous step using the **Display Name** as the mailbox name.

   h. Close the **POP3 Service** control panel.

Install the SharePoint Server

Follow these steps to install and configure the SharePoint server:

1. Install Microsoft Windows Server 2003, Standard or Enterprise Edition, with the following settings:

Parameter	Value
Computer Name	ogc
Administrator Password	!Pass1234
Domain Name	ourglobalcompany.com
IP Address	192.168.1.201
Subnet Mask	255.255.255.0
Default Gateway	192.168.1.200
Preferred DNS Server	192.168.1.200

2. Install Windows Server 2003 Service Pack 2. When prompted, restart the computer and log on as GLOBAL\Administrator.

3. Install and remove the Windows components.

   a. Choose **Start→Control Panel→Add Or Remove Programs.**

   b. Click **Add/Remove Windows Components.**

   c. Uncheck the **Internet Explorer Enhanced Security Configuration** check box.

   d. Select **Application Server** and click **Details.**

   e. Check the **ASP.NET** check box.

    f.   Select **Internet Information Services (IIS)** and click **Details.**

    g.   Verify that the **Common Files, Internet Information Services Manager, SMTP Service** and the **World Wide Web Service** check boxes are checked.

    h.   Verify that the **FrontPage 2002 Server Extensions** check box is not checked.

    i.   Click **OK** twice.

    j.   Click **Next.**

    k.   If necessary, insert the installation disk and browse for the required files.

    l.   Click **Finish.**

    m.   Close the **Add Or Remove Programs** control panel.

4.   Install Microsoft .NET Framework 3.0.

    a.   Download or copy the Microsoft .NET Framework 3.0 setup file to the server.

    b.   Click **Run.**

    c.   Check the **I have read and accept the terms of the licensing agreement** check box.

    d.   Click **Install.**

    e.   If necessary, click the icon in the taskbar to monitor the installation.

    f.   When the installation is complete, click **Exit.**

5.   Install Microsoft® Windows® SharePoint® Services 3.0.

    a.   Download or copy the Microsoft® Windows® SharePoint® Services 3.0 setup file to the server.

    b.   Check the **I Accept The Terms Of This Agreement** check box and click **Continue.**

    c.   Click **Basic.**

    d.   When the installation is complete, click **Close.**

    e.   Click **Next.**

    f.   To acknowledge that some services will be restarted, click **Yes.**

    g.   When the wizard is completed, click **Finish.**

    h.   The browser opens and displays **http://ogc/default.aspx** and you are logged on as GLOBAL\Administrator. Choose **Welcome→Sign Out,** and then click **Yes.**

6.   Configure Microsoft® Windows® SharePoint® Services 3.0.

    a.   Choose **Start→Administrative Tools→SharePoint 3.0 Central Administration.**

    b.   Click the **Operations** tab.

    c.   In the **Security Configuration,** section, click **Update Farm Administrator's Group.**

    d.   Click **New** and choose **Add Users.**

    e.   In the **Users/Groups** text box, type *global\domain admins* and click **OK.**

    f.   Click the **Operations** tab.

    g.   In the **Topology And Services** section, click **Outgoing Email Settings.**

    h.   For **Outbound SMTP Server,** type *ogc*

    i.   For **From Address,** type *central@ourglobalcompany.com*

    j.   For **Reply To Address,** type *central@ourglobalcompany.com* and click **OK.**

k.   Choose **Welcome GLOBAL\administrator→Sign Out,** and then click **Yes.**

7.   Configure the SMTP virtual server.

    a.   Choose **Start→Administrative Tools→Internet Information Services (IIS) Manager.**

    b.   If necessary, expand the local computer node.

    c.   Right-click **Default SMTP Virtual Server** and choose **Properties.**

    d.   Select the **Access** tab and then click **Relay.**

    e.   Select **All Except The List Below** and click **OK.**

    f.   Select the **Delivery** tab and then click **Advanced.**

    g.   For **Smart Host,** type *dc.ourglobalcompany.com* and click **OK** twice.

    h.   Close the Internet Information Services (IIS) Manager window.

Create a Top-Level Site for Each Student

To create a top-level site for each student:

1.   Choose **Start→Administrative Tools→SharePoint 3.0 Central Administration.**

2.   Click the **Application Management** tab.

3.   In the **SharePoint Web Application Management** section, click the **Create or extend Web application** option.

4.   In the **Adding a SharePoint Web Application** section, click the **Create a new Web application** option.

5.   On the **Create New Web Application** page, in the **Application Pool** section, in the **User name** text box, type *GLOBAL\Administrator* and in the **Password** text box, type *!Pass1234*

6.   Click **OK.**

7.   Choose **Start→Run.**

8.   In the **Open** text box, type *cmd*

9.   At the command prompt, type *iisreset/noforce*

10.   Close the command prompt window.

11.   On the **Application Created** page, click the **Create Site Collection** link.

12.   In the **Title** text box, type *Our Global Company*

13.   In the **Primary Site Collection Administrator** and **Secondary Site Collection Administrator** section, in the **User name** text box, type *GLOBAL\administrator*

14.   Click **OK.**

15.   Follow steps 3–14 to create individual top-level sites for all the class students as required.

Configure Permissions in the WSS Environment

Follow these steps to configure permissions for instructor and student access to the top level sites:

1.   Configure permissions for student access to the top level sites.

    a.   Open the top level site.

    b.   In the **Quick Launch** bar, click **People And Groups.**

    c.   On the **People And Groups: Our Global Company Members** page, click **New→ Add Users.**

    d.   On the **Add users: Our Global Company** page, in the **Add Users** section, click the **Browse** icon.

    e.   In the **Select People and Groups - Webpage Dialog** dialog box, in the **Find** text box, type *user* and click the **Search** icon.

    f.   Select **user01** for each of the top level site.

    g.   Similarly, add the users, **Susan Young, Bob Wheeler,** and **Maria Miller.**

    h.   Click **OK.**

    i.   In the **Give Permission** section, select the **Give users permission directly** option and check the **Full Control - Has full control** check box.

    j.   For **Personal Message,** type *Welcome to SharePoint. As a team site member, you can view, add, update, and delete items throughout the team site* and click **OK.**

    k.   Similarly, perform steps from 'a' to 'k' to configure permissions for users **user02** through **user12** (or as required) in their respective top level sites.

2.   Configure permissions for instructor access to the OGC top level site.

    a.   Open the ogc site.

    b.   In the **Quick Launch** bar, click **People And Groups.**

    c.   On the **People And Groups: Our Global Company Members** page, in the **Quick Launch** bar, click **Our Global Company Owners.**

    d.   On the **People And Groups: Our Global Company Owners** page, choose **New→ Add Users.**

    e.   On the **Add users: Our Global Company** page, in the **Add Users** section, click the **Browse** icon.

    f.   In the **Select People and Groups - Webpage Dialog** dialog box, in the **Find** text box, type *central* and click the **Search** icon.

    g.   Select **central.**

    h.   Similarly, add the users, **Susan Young, Bob Wheeler,** and **Maria Miller.**

    i.   Click **OK.**

    j.   On the **Add users: Our Global Company** page, click **OK.**

    k.   Choose **Welcome→Sign Out,** and then click **Yes.**

Setup the Instructor and Student Computers

Follow these steps to setup and configure the instructor and student computers:

1.   Install Windows XP Professional SP2 with the following settings.

- **Computer Name:**
  - Students: *computer01* through *computer12* (or more as required).
  - Instructor: *central*
- **Administrator Password:** *!Pass1234*
- **IP Address:**
  - Students: *192.168.1.1* through *192.168.1.12* (or as required)
  - Instructor: *192.168.1.101*

- **Subnet Mask:** *255.255.255.0*
- **Default Gateway:** *192.168.1.200*
- **Preferred DNS Server:** *192.168.1.200*
- **Domain:** *ourglobalcompany.com*

2. Assign the user as Administrator to the local machine.

    a. Choose **Start→Control Panel→Administrative Tools→Computer Management** console.

    b. Expand **Local Users And Groups.**

    c. Click **Groups.**

    d. Double-click **Administrators.**

    e. Click **Add.**

    f. Click **Advanced.**

    g. Click **Find Now.**

    h. Select the user name for the computer.

    i. Click **OK** three times.

    j. Close the Computer Management console.

3. Install and activate Microsoft Office 2007 Professional or Professional Plus.

4. Install and activate Microsoft Office SharePoint Designer 2007.

5. Install Microsoft .NET Framework 3.0.

6. On the course CD-ROM, run the 084721dd.exe self-extracting file located within. This will install a folder named **084721Data** on your C drive. This folder contains all the setup and data files that you will use to complete this course.

7. Log on to the GLOBAL domain as user## (password !Pass1234).

8. Configure Microsoft Office Outlook 2007 for instructor and student systems.

    a. Open Microsoft Office Outlook 2007.

    b. In the **Outlook 2007 Startup** wizard, click **Next.**

    c. Click **Next.**

    d. Verify that the correct email address is displayed and click **Next.**

    e. If necessary, check **Manually Configure Server Settings,** and provide the name, email address, outgoing and incoming mail server names (dc.ourglobalcompany.com), and ensure that the **POP3** option is selected. Click **Next.**

    f. Click **Next** and click **Finish.**

    g. Restart Microsoft Office Outlook 2007.

    h. When prompted to synchronize RSS feeds, click **Yes.**

    i. When prompted about desktop search, check the **Do not show this message again,** check box and click **No.**

    j. Choose **Actions→Junk E-mail→Junk E-mail Options.**

    k. In the **Junk E-mail Options** dialog box, select the **Safe Senders** tab.

    l. Click **Add** and in the **Add address or domain** dialog box, type *central@ourglobalcompany.com* and click **OK.**

    m. In the **Junk E-mail Options** dialog box, click **OK.**

n.   Log off.

9.   Similarly, configure Microsoft Office Outlook 2007 in the instructor's computer for the following user logins:

- Central
- Bob Wheeler
- Maria Miller
- Susan Young

Communicating Information to the Instructor and Students of the Class

The instructor and students in this class will need the following information to complete the course:

- The default top level site is http://ogc, which will be used by the instructor.
- Based on the port number (http://ogc:####), the instructor will allocate a separate top level site for each student.

List of Additional Files

Printed with each activity is a list of files students open to complete that activity. Many activities also require additional files that students do not open, but are needed to support the file(s) students are working with. These supporting files are included with the student data files on the course CD-ROM or data disk. Do not delete these files.

Visual Studio   Front Page 2003

Sharepoint Designer   Expression Web 2.0

1 | Getting Started with the SharePoint Designer Environment

Lesson Time: 30 minutes

Lesson Objectives:

In this lesson, you will familiarize yourself with the SharePoint Designer environment.

You will:

- Explore the SharePoint Designer interface.
- Customize the SharePoint Designer interface.
- Get help using the SharePoint Designer help feature.

Introduction

You have used Windows SharePoint Services to build intranet sites that meet your organization's requirements. There may be times when you would want to customize these sites and Microsoft Office SharePoint Designer helps you do that. In this lesson, you will familiarize yourself with the SharePoint Designer interface.

While working on any new application or software, you could potentially spend a significant amount of time searching for specific tools and options that you require to perform a task. You can prevent this by familiarizing yourself with the user interface of the software. Also, there may be times when you are unclear on how to accomplish a task or when there is an option on which you might need more information. An instruction manual or a user guide can be used as reference to assist with these kinds of issues. Similarly, there is an inbuilt help feature in Microsoft SharePoint Designer with which you can quickly access the help information you need.

TOPIC A

Explore the SharePoint Designer Interface

To get started with site customization or creation, you need to first familiarize yourself with the application you are going to work with. In this topic, you will explore the Microsoft Office SharePoint Designer interface.

When starting work with a new application, it is essential that you are familiar with its features and functions; else you may never be able to realize the full potential of the application. Its imperative that you familiarize yourself with the interface elements so that you can access and work with the tools and options you desire. Microsoft Office SharePoint Designer has a unique interface that you must be familiar with in order to customize or build SharePoint sites with ease.

The SharePoint Designer Environment

The SharePoint Designer environment is a customizable and an organized workspace, which makes it very easy to access the various options and tools in the software. It consists of five regions.

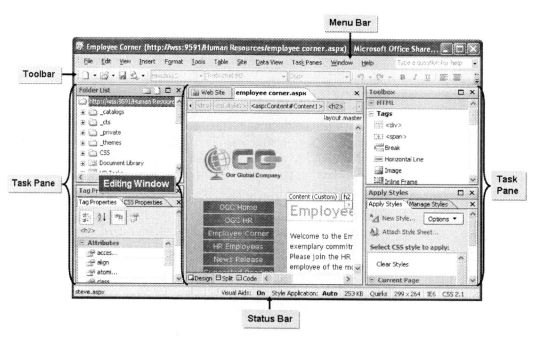

Figure 1-1: The five regions of the SharePoint Designer environment.

The following table lists the regions of the SharePoint Designer environment.

Interface Region	Description
The Menu bar	Displays the different menu items on the menu bar. Some of the commonly used menu items include **File, Edit, Format, Tools,** and **Task Panes.**
The toolbar	Consists of the frequently used buttons, which allow you to perform specific tasks in SharePoint Designer. The toolbar in SharePoint Designer is customized automatically, so as to display the recently used buttons, while the others are displayed in the **Toolbar Options** drop-down list. By default, the **Common** toolbar is displayed. SharePoint Designer offers various function-specific toolbars such as **Formatting, Code View,** and **Pictures.**
The editing window	Allows you to edit web pages. When a website is open, a web page tab is added to the editing window. You can view and edit a file in its code format by using the **Code** view, or design format by using the **Design** view. You can also split the editing window to edit the page in both code and design views at the same time by using the **Split** view.
The task pane	Makes it easier for the user to work with commands, modify a web page, and view information. Task panes provide options that enable you to perform specialized tasks such as managing styles, setting properties, and adding behaviors. By default, the **Folder List, Tag Properties, CSS Properties, Apply Styles, Manage Styles,** and **Toolbox** task panes are displayed. SharePoint Designer offers various other task panes such as **CSS Properties, Layout Tables, Behaviors,** and **Web Parts.**
The status bar	Displays information about the file that you are currently working on in the editing window. Provides information such as the visual aid status, browser type and version, schema, and file size.

The Menu Bar

The menu bar includes various menu items that provide you with options required to create a website. The following table lists the items listed on the menu bar of SharePoint Designer.

Menu	Provides Options To
File	Perform functions such as opening a new website, a new page, or an existing file, or saving, printing, and closing a website.
Edit	Modify or edit content on a web page.

Menu	Provides Options To
View	View a web page in different views and hide or display the desired toolbars.
Insert	Insert controls, bookmarks, pictures, files, and symbols, to a website.
Format	Format the contents of a website.
Tools	Enhance the quality of the website by checking for spelling, accessibility, and compatibility.
Table	Insert and modify tables.
Site	Manage a website, view the hyperlink structure, manage permission levels for users, and also to backup and restore a website.
Data View	Work with a database and display information from a database.
Task Panes	Hide or display the task pane that you need to work with.
Window	Manage multiple websites at the same time.
Help	Access SharePoint Designer help options.

The Common Toolbar

The **Common** toolbar is the default toolbar in SharePoint Designer. It contains some of the frequently used options such as style, alignment, and format.

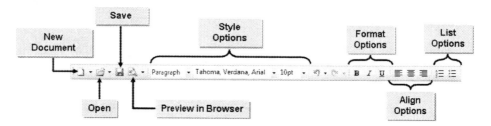

Figure 1-2: The options on the Common toolbar.

The following table lists the options on the **Common** toolbar.

Option	Description
New Document	Enables you to create a new web page. By using the **New Document** drop-down list, you can choose to create a new **Page, Web Site, SharePoint Content, HTML page, ASPX page, CSS, Workflow,** or a **Folder.**

Option	Description
Open	Allows you to open the **Open File** dialog box, using which you can open a desired web page. Using the **Open** drop-down list, you can open the **Open File** dialog box or the **Open Site** dialog box, which enables you to open a website. You can also open the **Open Workflow** dialog box, which enables you to open a workflow.
Save	Allows you to save a file. If you are saving the file for the first time, the **Save As**dialog box opens.
Preview in Browser	Allows you to preview the website in a browser window. The **Preview in Browser** drop-down list allows you to choose the browser in which you wish to preview the website. It also allows you to specify the size of the browser window.
Style options	Allows you to specify the style, font, and font size of the textual content.
Format options	Lets you format the selected text. You can bold, italicize, and underline text using the format options.
Align options	Enables you to align text to the right, left, or center of a page.
List options	Enables you to create numbered or bulleted lists on a web page.

Components of the Editing Window

The editing window is used for editing a web page. It consists of four components.

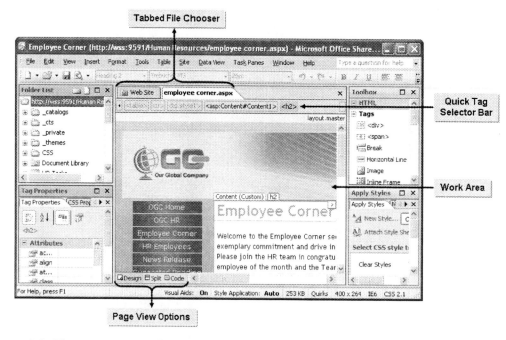

Figure 1-3: *The components of the SharePoint Designer editing window.*

The following table lists the components of the SharePoint Designer editing window.

Component	Description
The work area	The document window in which you actually work with the web page.
The page view options	The set of options that enable you to work on a web page in the code view, design view, or both.
The tabbed file chooser	The tabs in the editing window that enable you to navigate among multiple web pages. Each page is represented by a tab, clicking on which will display the specific web page.
The quick tag selector bar	The bar, which is present just below the tabbed file chooser enables you to edit tags within the work area.

The Folder List Task Pane

The **Folder List** task pane lists all the constituent elements of a website, listed in a nested tree-like structure. The first folder in this task pane is the root folder, below which all subfolders and other website elements, such as subsites, master pages, images, and web pages are listed. You can open and rename the files in the **Folder List** task pane. It also contains the **New Folder** button, which enables you to create a new folder, and a **New Page** button, which enables you to create a new web page.

> By default, the **New Page** button creates a new .htm page.

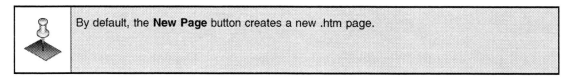

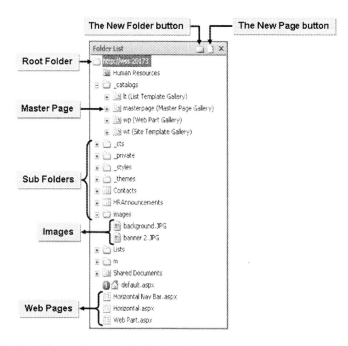

Figure 1-4: *The Folder List task pane displaying the website elements.*

Types of Page Views

SharePoint Designer gives designers an option to work in the design view of a page or with the code view, or with both.

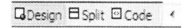

Figure 1-5: *The different page views in SharePoint Designer.*

How to Explore the SharePoint Designer Interface

Procedure Reference: Open a SharePoint Site

To open a SharePoint site:

1. Choose **Start→All Programs→Microsoft Office→Microsoft Office SharePoint Designer 2007** to launch the application.

2. Display the **Open Site** dialog box.
   - Choose **File→Open Site.**
   - Or, on the **Common** toolbar, from the **Open** drop-down list, select **Open Site.**

3. Open the site.
   - In the **Open Site** dialog box, navigate to the desired web site and click **Open.**
   - Or, in the **Site name** text box, type the URL of the site you want to open.

4. Open a web page in the website.
   - In the **Folder List** task pane, double-click a web page.
   - Or, on the **Web Site** tab, double-click a web page.

5. If necessary, choose **File→Close.**

Procedure Reference: Explore the SharePoint Designer Interface

To explore the SharePoint Designer interface:

1. Open the desired web page.

2. Explore the various user interface elements.
   - On the menu bar, click on a menu item to view its menu options.
   - On the **Common** toolbar, mouse over the button to view its corresponding tool tip description.
   - Change the view of the web page.
     - On the view bar, click **Design** to view the web page in the design view.
     - Click **Code** to view the web page in the code view.
     - Click **Split** to view the web page in a split window displaying the page in both the design view and the code view.
   - Select a task pane tab to activate the tab in the task pane.
   - Mouse over the status bar sections and observe the details displayed in their respective tool tip.

ACTIVITY 1-1

Exploring the SharePoint Designer Interface

Scenario:

You are planning to customize an existing WSS site and also create a subsite for your company. Your organization has recently provided all web designers with the SharePoint Designer application. However, before you start creating the web page, you wish to get familiar with the user interface.

What You Do	How You Do It
1. Open the Windows SharePoint Services site.	a. Choose **Start→All Programs→Microsoft Office→Microsoft Office SharePoint Designer 2007.**
	b. In the **User Name** message box, click **OK** to accept the default values.
	c. In the **Microsoft Office SharePoint Designer** dialog box, uncheck the **Always perform this check when starting SharePoint Designer** check box and click **Yes.**
	d. If necessary, in the **Welcome to the 2007 Microsoft Office system** dialog box, click **OK.**
	e. Choose **File→Open Site.**
	f. In the **Open Site** dialog box, in the **Site name** text box, click and type *http:// [sitename]* and click **Open.**
	g. If necessary, in the **Connect to ogc** dialog box, in the **User name** text box, type your login name.
	h. If necessary, in the **Password** text box, click and type *!Pass1234* and then click **OK.**
	i. In the **Folder List** task pane, double-click **default.aspx** to open the home page of the website.

2. **Which option in the editing window allows you to navigate among multiple web pages?**

    a) The work area

    b) Page views

    c) The tabbed file chooser

    d) The quick tag selector bar

---

3. Compare the different view modes.

    a. On the view bar, click **Code.**

    b. Observe that the **default.aspx** page is displayed in the code format.

    c. On the view bar, click **Split.**

    d. Observe that the **default.aspx** page is displayed in both the code and design views.

    e. On the view bar, click **Design** to restore the design view.

---

4. **Which view enables you to see the changes happening on the web page as you work on its code?**

    a) The Code view

    b) The Design view

    c) The Split view

    d) The page view

---

5. View the options in the **Manage Styles** task pane.

    a. In the **Apply Styles** task pane, select the **Manage Styles** tab.

    b. Observe that the **Manage Styles** task pane and its options are displayed.

---

6. View the web page details using the status bar options.

    a. On the status bar, move the mouse pointer over the sections you desire to view their description.

    b. Choose **File→Close** to close the **default.aspx** page.

TOPIC B

Customize the SharePoint Designer Interface

You have explored the SharePoint Designer environment. The default interface of a software might not always be very comfortable to work with. In this topic, you will customize the SharePoint Designer interface.

The default interface settings of an application may not always suit your specific requirements. The tools and panes that you need may not be present in the interface, or there may be tools that you do not need. Customizing the interface elements ensures that you can easily access those tools that you use frequently and also that your application environment is devoid of other unwanted tools and commands.

The Customize Dialog Box

The **Customize** dialog box allows you to customize a toolbar. It consists of the **Toolbars, Commands,** and the **Options** tabs.

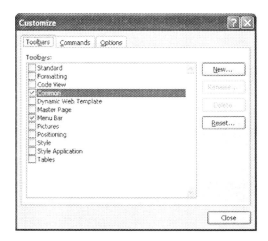

Figure 1-6: The Customize dialog box with the Toolbars tab selected.

The table below describes the functions of these tabs.

Tab	Enables You To
Toolbars	Create a new toolbar, rename, or delete an existing toolbar, and also reset a toolbar to its default settings.
Commands	Choose and add commands to a toolbar; these commands are grouped under various categories. It also enables you to rearrange and modify the properties of the commands on a toolbar.

Tab	Enables You To
Options	Specify the size of the icon on the toolbar. It also enables you to specify any screen tips or shortcut keys for the selected command. The **Reset menu and toolbar usage data** button on the **Options** tab enables you to reset the menu bar and toolbars.

How to Customize the SharePoint Designer Interface

Procedure Reference: Reposition the Menu Bar

To reposition the menu bar:

1. Choose **Start→Microsoft Office SharePoint Designer 2007** to open the application.
2. Place the mouse pointer on the left corner of the menu bar.
3. When the mouse pointer changes to a four-headed arrow, reposition the menu bar as desired.
   - Drag toward the editing window to float it.
   - Drag to the left corner of the window to dock it on the left margin of the interface.
   - Drag to the right corner of the window to dock it on the right margin of the interface.
   - Drag to the bottom of the window to dock it at the base of the interface.
4. If necessary, choose **File→Close.**

Procedure Reference: Customize a Toolbar

To customize a toolbar:

1. Display the desired toolbar.
   - Right-click the menu bar or the toolbar region and choose the desired toolbar.
   - Or, choose **View→Toolbars→*[Toolbar name]*** and then choose the desired toolbar.
2. Customize the toolbar.
   - Position the toolbar at the desired location.
     - Place the mouse pointer on the border of the toolbar and, when the mouse pointer changes to a four-headed arrow, drag the floating toolbar anywhere you want on the interface.
     - Place the mouse pointer on the border of the toolbar and, when the mouse pointer changes to a four-headed arrow, drag the floating toolbar and dock it on any side of the interface.
   - Place the mouse pointer on the border of the toolbar and, when the mouse pointer changes to a double-headed arrow, drag to resize.
   - Add or remove buttons on a toolbar.
     - a. In the title bar of the toolbar, from the **Toolbar Options** drop-down list, select **Add or Remove Buttons.**

b. From the **Add or Remove Buttons** drop-down list, choose the desired option, either the *[Toolbar Name]* option or the **Customize** option to add or remove the toolbar buttons.

- Check the buttons you wish to add.
- Uncheck the buttons you wish to remove.
- Click **Reset Toolbar** to restore the default toolbar buttons.

3. If necessary, close the toolbar.

- In the title bar, click the **Close** button.
- Right-click the toolbar and on the shortcut menu, uncheck the toolbar.
- Or, choose **View→Toolbars** and uncheck the toolbar that you want to close.

Types of Toolbars

The following table lists the different toolbars available in the SharePoint Designer.

Toolbar	*Description*
Standard	Displays common options such as **Save, Print,** and **Insert Table.**
Formatting	Displays the formatting options such as those used for alignment, font, and listing.
Code View	Displays options that allow you to edit the web page directly in the source code view.
Common	Displays a combination of commonly used options from all other toolbars.
Dynamic Web Template (DWT)	Displays the options used to work on the DWT.
Master Page	Displays the options used to work on the master page.
Pictures	Displays the options used to work on pictures on a website.
Positioning	Displays the options used to position the elements on a website.
Style	Displays options to work with styles, create a new style sheet, or attach an existing one.
Style Application	Enables you to set the style application mode.
Tables	Displays options used to work with tables.

Procedure Reference: Create a Custom Toolbar

To create a custom toolbar:

1. Display the **Customize** dialog box.

   ● In the title bar of the toolbar, in the **Toolbar Options** drop-down list, choose **Add or Remove Buttons→Customize.**

   ● Right-click the menu bar or the toolbar region and choose **Customize.**

2. On the **Toolbars** tab, click **New** to display the **New Toolbar** dialog box.

3. In the **Toolbar name** text box, type a desired name and click **OK** to display the floating toolbar.

4. In the **Customize** dialog box, select the **Commands** tab.

5. In the **Categories** list, select the desired category.

   Some of the main categories listed are **File, Edit, Insert, Table, Tools, Task Panes,** and **Macros.**

6. In the **Commands** list, select a desired command, and drag the command to the floating toolbar.

7. If necessary, repeat steps 5 and 6 to add the required commands to the custom toolbar.

8. Click the title bar of the toolbar and drag to an appropriate location.

9. Click the **Close** button to close the **Customize** dialog box.

10. If necessary, choose **View→Toolbars→[customized toolbar]** to open it.

Procedure Reference: Customize a Task Pane

To customize a task pane:

1. Choose **Task Panes→[Task pane name]** to display the desired task pane.

2. Customize the task pane.

   ● Right-click the title bar and select **Float** to float the task pane.

   ● Click the title bar and drag to an appropriate location to relocate the task pane.

   ● Place the mouse pointer on a task pane tab and drag it toward another to group task panes.

    When you have multiple tabs grouped in a single task pane, you can use the **Scroll Left** and **Scroll Right** buttons to navigate between them.

   ● Click the **Maximize Window** button to maximize the task pane.

   ● Place the mouse pointer on the border of the task pane and when the mouse pointer changes to a double-headed arrow, drag to resize.

3. If desired, choose **Task Panes→Reset Workspace Layout** to restore the default task panes.

4. If necessary, in the title bar of the task pane, click the **Close** button to close the task pane.

Types of Task Panes

The following table lists the different task panes provided by SharePoint Designer.

Task Pane	Description
Folder List	Displays the folder structure of the website.
Navigation	Displays the hierarchical structure of the website. It enables you to arrange the pages in your site and also to customize the navigation links of your website.
Tag Properties	Enables you to modify the set attributes and values of the currently active tag.
CSS Properties	Enables you to quickly work with all the styles that can be applied to a selected element.
Layout Tables	Provides tools that will enable you to modify layout tables.
Apply Styles	Enables you to work with styles.
Manage Styles	Enables you to move styles from an external CSS to an internal CSS or vice versa.
Behaviors	Enables you to add behavior of elements.
Layers	Enables you to list and create layers on the current web page.
Toolbox	Enables you to drag HTML elements from controls and ASP.NET controls to your page.
Data Source Library	Enables you to work with database connections on your website.
Data Source Details	Displays the content of XML files in a hierarchy.
Conditional Formatting	Enables you to customize XML data in data view.
Find Data Source	Enables you to search for a data source in your website.
Web Parts	Enables you to work with Web Parts on your website.
Find 1	Enables you to search multiple pages at a time.
Find 2	Enables you to perform an additional search at the same time.
Accessibility	Enables you to generate accessibility reports.
Compatibility	Enables you to generate compatibility reports.
Hyperlinks	Enables you to manage the hyperlinks on your website.
CSS Reports	Enables you to manage style errors or usage of CSS on a website.

Task Pane	Description
Clip Art	Enables you to search for, add, and organize clip art, images, audio files, and video files to your website.
Clipboard	Enables you to temporarily store the data that is being transferred from one document to the other via copy/paste functions.
Contributor	Enables you to set the editing restrictions for your site.

ACTIVITY 1-2

Customizing the SharePoint Designer Interface

Before You Begin:

Ensure that the **ogc** website from the previous activity is open.

Scenario:

As you are exploring the interface, you find that the SharePoint Designer provides you with various options to modify the SharePoint Designer environment. You decide to familiarize yourself with the customization features and practice customizing a few interface elements, so that when you are working on real-time projects, you would be able to easily customize the environment to suit your specific needs.

What You Do	How You Do It
1. Display and reposition the **Pictures** toolbar.	a. Choose **View→Toolbars→Pictures.**
	b. Drag the **Pictures** toolbar and dock it below the left end of the **Common** toolbar.

	c. Place the mouse pointer on the left corner of the **Pictures** toolbar till it changes to a four-headed arrow and drag the toolbar to the editing window to float it.
	d. On the **Pictures** toolbar, click the **Close** button.
2. Close the **Tag Properties** and **Folder List** task panes.	a. In the **Tag Properties** task pane, click the **Close** button.
	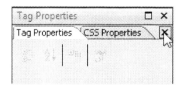
	b. Close the **Folder List** task pane.

3. Display and reposition the **Layers** task pane.

    a. Choose **Task Panes→Layers.**

    b. Observe that the **Layers** task pane is added to the bottom-right corner of the window.

    c. Place the mouse pointer on the top edge of the **Layers** task pane group title bar till it changes to a double-headed arrow and drag upward by an inch to resize the task pane group.

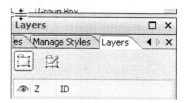

    d. Right-click the **Layers** task pane group title bar and select **Float.**

    e. Place the mouse pointer in the **Layers** task pane group title bar and drag toward the editing window to float it.

    f. Drag the floating **Layers** task pane group toward the **CSS Properties** task pane to group them.

4. Reset the workspace layout.

    a. Choose **Task Panes→Reset Workspace Layout** to restore the default task panes.

    b. Choose **File→Close Site.**

ACTIVITY 1-3

Creating a Custom Toolbar

Scenario:

While exploring the SharePoint Designer interface, you find certain commands that you might use frequently. For ease of access, you decide to group them on a separate toolbar.

What You Do	How You Do It
1. Create a custom toolbar.	a. Right-click the menu bar region and choose **Customize.**
	b. Select the **Toolbars** tab.
	c. On the **Toolbars** tab, click **New** to display the **New Toolbar** dialog box.
	d. In the **Toolbar name** text box, type *My Toolbar* and click **OK.**
	e. Observe that **My Toolbar** is displayed as a floating toolbar.

2. Add commands to the toolbar.

a. In the **Customize** dialog box, select the **Commands** tab.

b. In the **Commands** list box, scroll down and drag the **SharePoint Content** command out of the dialog box to **My Toolbar.**

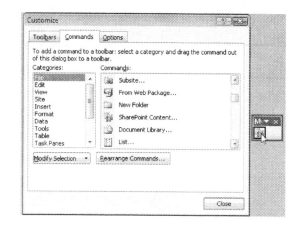

c. In the **Categories** list box, select **Task Panes.**

d. In the **Commands** list box, drag the **Layout Tables** command out of the dialog box to **My Toolbar.**

e. Add the **CSS Properties** command to **My Toolbar.**

f. In the **Customize** dialog box, click the **Close** button.

g. Drag the **My Toolbar** toolbar and dock it below the left end of the **Common** toolbar.

TOPIC C

Get Help in SharePoint Designer

You have explored the SharePoint Designer interface and also customized the interface to suit your needs. Before you start working on it, you would like to have some in-depth knowledge of a specific task. In this topic, you will use SharePoint Designer's help feature to find out more about a certain task.

You have just started with SharePoint Designer. You find that you are not able to proceed further with a certain task, and you need some help in understanding the functionality. There is no one in the office available to help you. What will you do? These are the moments when you will find SharePoint Designer's help feature useful.

The SharePoint Designer Help Feature

The *SharePoint Designer Help* feature acts as a central location where you can learn how to work with the software and obtain product support information. The **SharePoint Designer Help** home page contains a list of topics on SharePoint Designer. You can either browse through the various topics listed, or search for a specific topic using the **Search** text box. You can further refine your search by specifying the type of help content that you require from **SharePoint Designer Help.** It can be help content on Microsoft Office Online, or help content on your computer. You can also use the specific tools that are found on the **SharePoint Designer Help** navigation bar to browse through the **Help** window.

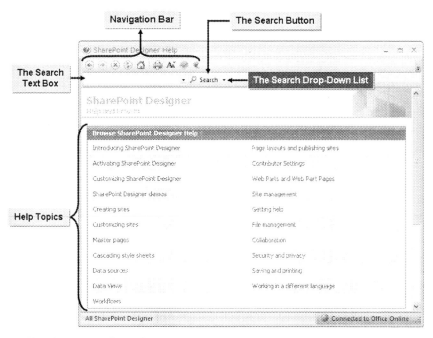

Figure 1-7: *The features of the SharePoint Designer Help window.*

To browse through **SharePoint Designer Help,** you can use the buttons on the navigation bar.

Button	Description
Back and **Forward**	
	Helps you navigate between the help pages you visited.
Stop	
	Stops the current page from loading or reloading.
Refresh	
	Reloads the information on the currently displayed page.
Home	
	Returns you to the **SharePoint Designer Help's** home page.
Print	
	Prints the current help page.
Change Font Size	
	Changes the font size of the contents of the pages.
Show Table of Contents	
	Displays the contents of the help files in a pane on the left side of the page.
Keep On Top	
	Keeps the **SharePoint Designer Help** window on top of the SharePoint Designer window.

The Help Menu

The **Help** menu provides the users with options to activate the product, and to know about the license information of the product. It also has links to the Microsoft website wherein the user can find information related to the latest software updates, the Microsoft privacy statement, and product support.

How to Use the SharePoint Designer Help Feature

Procedure Reference: Use the SharePoint Designer Help Feature

To use the **SharePoint Designer Help** feature:

1. Choose **Help→Microsoft Office SharePoint Designer Help.**
2. Get the desired form of help and support.

    *   In the **Browse SharePoint Designer Help** list, click a suitable help and support document and view the contents.
    *   Search for support documents by keyword.

        a. In the **Search** text box, click and type the search keyword.
        b. From the **Search** drop-down list, select a desired search area.
        c. Click the **Search** button to start searching.
        d. Click a suitable help and support document and view the contents.

    *   Or, on the **SharePoint Designer Help** home page, in the **More on Office Online** section, click a desired option to search for updates, templates, or training courses related to SharePoint Designer.

3. If necessary, click the **Change Font Size** button to change the font size of the contents of the page.
4. If necessary, use the **Forward** and **Back** buttons to navigate between pages.
5. If necessary, click the **Home** icon to go back to the home page of **SharePoint Designer Help.**

ACTIVITY 1-4

Getting Help on SharePoint Designer

Scenario:

As you continue with your exploration of SharePoint Designer, you want to know how to go about adding a web page to a site. You are not sure of how to do this task.

What You Do	How You Do It
1. Access **SharePoint Designer Help**.	a. Choose **Help→Microsoft Office SharePoint Designer Help**.
	b. Maximize the **SharePoint Designer Help** window.
	c. In the **SharePoint Designer Help** window, click the **Show me offline help from my computer** link.
	d. Observe the topics listed in the **SharePoint Designer Help and How-to** screen.
2. Search for help files on adding pages to a SharePoint site.	a. In the **Search** text box, click and type *Adding pages to a SharePoint site*
	b. Click the **Search** drop-down list.
	c. Verify that in the **Search** drop-down list, in the **Content from this computer** section, **SharePoint Designer Help** is selected.
	d. Click the **Search** button to start searching.
	e. On the search results page that is displayed, click the **Add a page to a SharePoint site** link to view the document.
	f. Close the **SharePoint Designer Help** window.

Lesson 1 Follow-up

In this lesson, you familiarized yourself with the basic elements of the Microsoft Office SharePoint Designer environment. You also used the SharePoint Designer help feature to get information on topics that you weren't familiar with. Familiarity with the SharePoint Designer interface makes it easier for you to work and get started with developing or customizing a website.

1. **In your opinion, which of the tools or features in the SharePoint Designer interface would be handy in speeding up the task of building a web page?**

2. **What according to you are the advantages of customizing the SharePoint Designer environment?**

2 | Creating a Subsite

Lesson Time: 1 hour(s), 10 minutes

Lesson Objectives:

In this lesson, you will create a new subsite.

You will:

- Create a page layout.
- Create a master page.
- Modify the master page layout.

Introduction

You have explored the SharePoint Designer environment and you are now ready to create a subsite and structure it. In this lesson, you will create a subsite and design a layout for the site.

It might be confusing for people to work on a SharePoint site if all the departments in the company were to use the same site for collaboration and interaction. Having a site for each department in an organization enables collaboration and makes interaction with your colleagues more efficient and streamlined.

TOPIC A
Create a Page Layout

Now that you've explored and customized the SharePoint Designer environment, you're ready to create your own site. Before you start developing web pages, the first step is to design the layout of the page. In this topic, you will create a blank subsite and design the layout.

It's easy to end up with a cluttered and difficult-to-navigate web page when you add elements to it on an ad hoc basis. Tables are the easiest and most common way of positioning elements on a web page. Using layout tables, you'll be able to exactly position components on a page. By spending a little up-front time planning a page layout, you'll have more professional-looking web pages.

Site Collections

A *site collection* is a collection of websites on a web server. Each site collection consists of a top-level site and one or more subsites. The *top-level site* is the main site where the administrator settings for a site collection are changed. The *subsite* is a website that is stored inside the top-level site. Both the top-level site and subsites can contain subsites, lists, documents, discussions, and surveys.

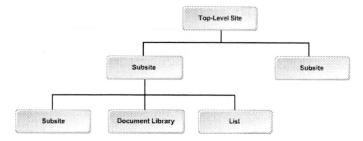

Figure 2-1: *An illustration of a site collection.*

Administrator Settings for a Subsite

By default, all subsites in a site collection will have the same administrator setting as set for the top-level site. However, you can change the administrator settings for each of the subsites, independent of the permissions of the top-level site.

Types of Web Pages

There are different types of web pages that help you to display information on the website. Web pages differ from each other based on their scripting languages. Some of the commonly used web pages are ASP, HTML, and, CSS.

Type Of Web Pages	Description
ASPX	ASPX is an ASP.NET file that is based on a set of HTML codes, designed to support interactivity on a web page.

Type Of Web Pages	Description
CSS	CSS pages are pages based on Cascading Style Sheets that is used to create structurally advanced, fluid design websites. These pages provide an immense amount of flexibility in terms of design.
HTML	HTML pages are based on the HyperText Markup Language (HTML).
CFML	CFML pages are pages based on the ColdFusion Markup Language, which helps you to create interactive web pages and sophisticated Internet applications.

The New Dialog Box

The **New** dialog box allows you to create a new page or a website. It consists of the **Page, Web Site,** and the **SharePoint Content** tabs.

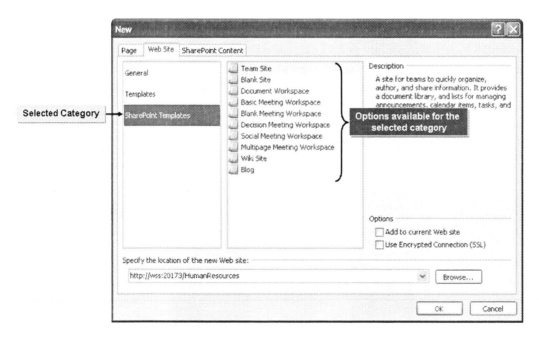

Figure 2-2: *The options in the Web Site tab of the New dialog box.*

The following table lists the options in the **New** dialog box.

Tab	Description
Page	Provides options that enable you to create a new page. • **General:** Enables you to create default pages such as HTML, ASPX, CSS, Javascript, and XML. • **ASP.NET:** Enables you to create ASP pages such as the ASP.NET page, Master Page, and Web User Control. • **CSS Layouts:** Enables you to create CSS pages with different layout designs. • **Frames Pages:** Enables you to create frames pages with different layout designs. It also contains sections to preview the page, view its description, and set the page editor options.
Web Site	Contains two categories, **General** and **SharePoint Templates,** which enable you to create a new subsite. The **General** category enables you to create new websites from scratch, while the **SharePoint Templates** category contains professionally designed SharePoint site templates that can be customized. It also contains the sections using which you can navigate to the required location where you want to create the new subsite, view the description of the selected site, add the site to the current website, and use encrypted connection.
SharePoint Content	Contains the **Lists, Document Libraries, Surveys,** and **Workflow** categories. This tab is displayed only when a SharePoint site is kept open. • The **Lists** category enables you to add new lists such as the calendar, announcements, links, and tasks. • The **Document Libraries** category enables you to add new libraries such as document and picture. • The **Surveys** category enables you to add a new survey. • The **Workflow** category enables you to create a new workflow. It also contains sections where you can view the description and specify a name for the selected item.

The Page Properties Dialog Box

The **Page Properties** dialog box contains several tabs that provide you with options to set the properties of a page.

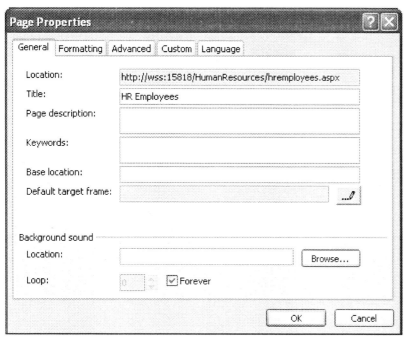

Figure 2-3: The tabs in the Page Properties dialog box.

The following table lists the options in the **Page Properties** dialog box.

Tab	Description
General	Provides options that enable you to view the location of the page and set or edit page properties such as title, description, keywords, background, and sound.
Formatting	Provides options that enable you to set or change the formatting properties on the page. The formatting properties include the background color, background images, text color, and hyperlink color.
Advanced	Provides options that enable you to set or edit the margins of a page. It contains text boxes where you can set the top, left, bottom, and right margins for the page.
Custom	Provides options that enable you to set the system and user variables through the use of the HTML code.
Language	Provides options that enable you to specify a language for the page.

Layouts

A *layout* is a framework that helps you to control the placement of elements on a web page. In SharePoint Designer, you can create layouts using layout tables, frames pages, and CSS layouts.

Layout Option	Description
Layout Table	A layout type that consists of tables, which are created using HTML codes. These tables are not visible on the website and are mainly used for structuring the web page content.
Frames Pages	A layout type in which each portion/compartment of the layout is an individual web page. Web pages that are created using frames have a faster download time as only a part of the page needs to be updated.
CSS Layouts	A layout type that is created using Cascading Style Sheets (CSS). CSS layouts enable you to exactly position elements on a web page and are also supported by older versions of browsers.

The Layout Tables Task Pane

The **Layout Tables** task pane enables you to design the layout of a web page. You can either create customized layout tables and cells or choose a layout from a list of predefined layout tables. It also provides options to change the properties of the selected layout table.

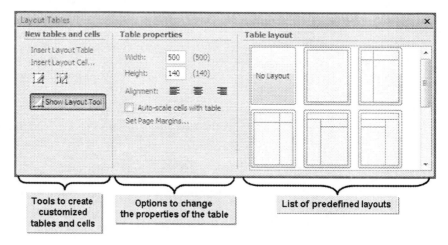

Figure 2-4: *The options in the Layout Tables task pane, using which you can create layout tables.*

Layout Tools

The layout tools are displayed when a table is selected. These tools enable you to resize the layout table and cells.

Tool	*Description*
Resize handles	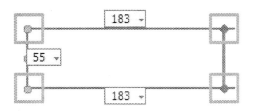
	The resize handles appear on the border of the layout table and enable you to resize the table or the cells. Pressing the **Alt** key and dragging the resize handle enable you to move the border in smaller increments.
Row height label	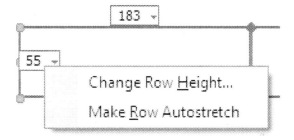
	The options in the row height label drop-down list enable you to define the row height of a cell.
	• The **Change Row height** option: Displays the **Row Properties** dialog box, where you can specify the row height, clear the height that contradicts with the specified height, make row autostretch, and use an image to act as a place holder.
	• The **Make Row Autostretch** option: Enables you to stretch a row automatically.

Tool	Description
Column width label	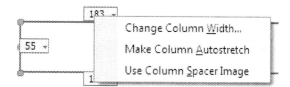

The options in the column width label drop-down list enable you to define the column width of a cell.

- The **Change Column Width** option: Displays the **Column Properties** dialog box, where you can specify the column width, clear the column width that contradicts with the specified width, make column autostretch, and use an image to act as a place holder.

- The **Make Column Autostretch** option: Enables you to make a column stretch automatically.

- The **Use column Spacer Image** option: Enables you to use an image to act as a placeholder.

The Tables Toolbar

The **Tables** toolbar contains many tool groups that enable you to create and modify tables on a web page.

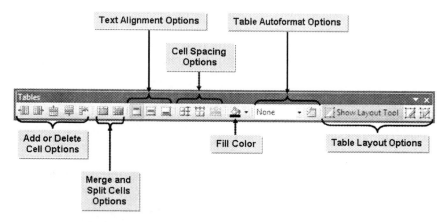

Figure 2-5: The tool groups on the Tables toolbar.

The following table lists the options in the **Tables** toolbar.

Tool Group	*Description*
Add or delete cell options	Contains options to add and delete cells in a table.
	• **Column to the Left:** Adds a new column to the left of the selected cell.
	• **Column to the Right:** Adds a new column to the right of the selected cell.
	• **Row Above:** Adds a new row above the selected cell.
	• **Row Below:** Adds a new row below the selected cell.
	• **Delete Cells:** Deletes the selected cells.
Merge and Split cells options	Contains options to merge a set of cells or split a cell into multiple rows or columns.
	• **Merge Cells:** Merges the selected cells.
	• **Split Cells:** Displays the **Split Cells** dialog box where you can specify the desired number of rows or columns.
Text alignment options	Provides options to align the text in a cell.
	• **Align Top:** Aligns the text within the selected cell to the top.
	• **Center Vertically:** Aligns the text within the selected cell in the center.
	• **Align Bottom:** Aligns the text within the selected cell to the bottom.
Cell spacing options	Contains options to resize the cell's spacing.
	• **Distribute Rows Evenly:** Resizes the selected row of cells evenly.
	• **Distribute Columns Evenly:** Resizes the selected column of cells evenly.
	• **AutoFit to Contents:** Resizes the selected cell based on the content added to it.
The Fill color option	Selects a color from the **Fill Color (Auto)** drop-down list. This color will be added as a background color for the selected cell.
Table autoformat options	Provides options to autoformat a table.
	• **Table AutoFormat Combo:** Selects an autoformat option from a list.
	• **Table AutoFormat:** Opens the **Table AutoFormat** dialog box where you can select an autoformat option and also apply formatting to the selected option.

Tool Group	Description
Table layout options	Provides options to design the layout of the table. ● **Show Layout Tool:** View the table in the layout mode. ● **Draw Layout Table:** Draw a layout table by selecting this option and clicking and dragging the insertion point on the page. ● **Draw Layout Cell:** Draw a layout cell by selecting this option and clicking and dragging the insertion point within the layout table.

The Table Properties Dialog Box

The **Table Properties** dialog box allows you to modify the properties of a table.

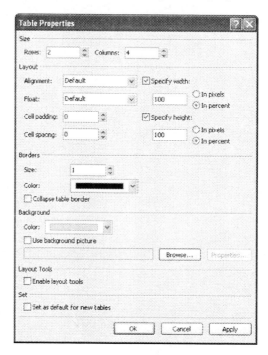

Figure 2-6: The options in the Table Properties dialog box.

The following table lists the options in the **Table Properties** dialog box.

Table Property	Description
Size	Provides options to set the number of rows and columns in the table.

Table Property	Description
Layout	Provides options to set the layout.
	• **Alignment:** Determines whether items placed in the table's cells are aligned left, right, or center within the cell.
	• **Specify Width:** Allows you to set the table's width in pixels or as a percentage of the window width. If not enabled, the browser sets the table width to 100 percent of its window size.
	• **Specify Height:** Allows you to set the table's height in pixels or as a percentage of the window height. Table height is not set by default.
	• **Cell Padding:** Determines the amount of space between the cell border and the content region of the cell.
	• **Cell Spacing:** Determines the amount of space between cells.
Borders	Provides options to set the border properties of the table.
	• **Size:** Determines the thickness of the table's border.
	• **Color:** Sets the border color for the table.
	• **Collapse table border:** Enables you to remove the border of the table when this check box is checked.
Background	Provides options to set background for the table.
	• **Color:** Enables you to select a color from the **Color** drop-down list or open the **More Colors** dialog box. It also contains options to set the background image for the table.
	• **Use background picture:** Enables you to add a background image to the table.
Layout Tools	Provides the **Enable layout tools** check box, which allows you to enable or disable the layout tools in the table.
Set	Provides the **Set as default for new tables** check box, which enables you to set the selected table properties as default for new tables.

The Cell Properties Dialog Box

The **Cell Properties** dialog box allows you to set the properties for an individual cell or for multiple cells in a table.

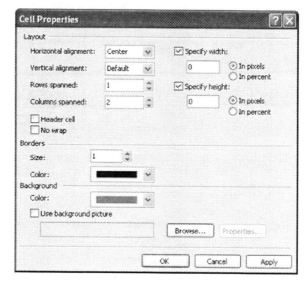

Figure 2-7: The options in the Cell Properties dialog box.

The following table lists the options in the **Cell Properties** dialog box.

Cell Property	Description
Layout	Provides options to set the layout.
	• **Horizontal Alignment:** Enables you to control the horizontal position of the contents of a cell. The options are **Default, Left, Right, Center,** and **Justify.**
	• **Vertical Alignment:** Enables you to control the vertical position of the contents of a cell. The options are **Top, Middle, Baseline,** and **Bottom.**
	• **Specify Height** and **Specify Width:** Enables you to specify the height and width of the cell. If you do not provide the value, the browser determines the cell's size.
	• **Rows Spanned** and **Columns Spanned:** Enables you to allow individual cells to occupy more than one row or column.
	• **Header Cell:** Enables you to set the cell as a header cell so that it's content is bold and centered.
	• **No Wrap:** Provides options to enable or disable the wrapping property for a cell.

Cell Property	Description
Borders	Provides options to set the borders for a cell.
	• **Size:** Enables you to set the size for the cell's border line.
	• **Color:** Enables you to set the color of the cell's border line.
Background	Provides options to set the color or image of the cell's background.

The More Colors Dialog Box

The **More Colors** dialog box provides additional options to add and modify text, backgrounds, and border colors on a web page.

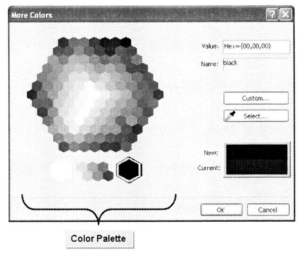

Color Palette

Figure 2-8: The options in the More Colors dialog box.

The following table lists the options in the **More Colors** dialog box.

Option	Allows You To
Color Palette	Select the desired color from a set of colors.
Value	Display the hex value of the selected color. You can also type the hex value of the desired color.
Name	Display the name of the selected color.
Custom	Open the **Color** dialog box where you can add customized colors.
Select	Select the desired color from anywhere in the environment.

Option	Allows You To
New/Current	View the current color and the newly selected color. This helps you to easily find the differences between the two colors. You can also shift back to the original color by clicking in the **New/Current** color field.

How to Create a Page Layout

Procedure Reference: Create a Subsite

To create a subsite:

1. Open a site in Microsoft Office SharePoint Designer.
2. Display the **New** dialog box.
   - Choose **File→New→Web Site.**
   - Or, on the **Common** toolbar, from the **New Document** drop-down list, select **Web Site.**
3. If necessary, in the **New** dialog box, on the **Web Site** tab, in the left pane, select the desired category.
   - In the left pane, select the **General** category and in the middle pane, select the desired type of subsite.
     - Select **One Page Web Site** to create a subsite with the default master page and a default ASPX page.
     - Or, select **Empty Web Site** to create a subsite with the default master page.
   - Select **SharePoint Templates,** if necessary, browse to the WSS site, and then in the middle section, select the type of subsite you want to create.

     Subsite types include **Team Site, Blank Site, Document Workspace, Wiki Site,** and **Blog.**
4. In the **Specify the location of the new Web site** section, click **Browse.**
5. In the **New Web Site Location** dialog box, navigate to the desired location.
6. Select the folder where you want to create the subsite and click **Open.**
7. If necessary, add folders to the website.
   - Choose **File→New→Folder** and type the desired name for the folder and press **Enter.**
   - On the **Web Site** tab, right-click and choose **New→Folder.** Type the desired name for the folder and press **Enter.**
   - On the **Common** toolbar, from the **New Document** drop-down list, select **New Folder.**
   - Or, right-click in the **Folder List** task pane and choose **New→Folder.** Type the desired name for the folder and press **Enter.**

You can use the **New Folder** button in the **Folder List** task pane or on the **Web Site** tab to create a new folder and specify a name for the folder.

Procedure Reference: Create a New Web Page

To create a new web page:

1. Open the desired website.
2. Create a new web page.
   - Choose **File→New→Page** and in the **New** dialog box, in the middle pane, select the desired type of page and click **OK.**
   - On the **Common** toolbar, click the **New Document** button.
   - Choose **File→New→ASPX** to create a new ASPX page.
   - Or, click the **New Document** drop-down arrow, choose **Page,** and in the **New** dialog box, in the middle pane, select the desired type of page and click **OK.**
3. Save the web page.
   a. Display the **Save As** dialog box.
      - Choose **File→Save As.**
      - Choose **File→Save.**
      - Or, on the **Common** toolbar, click the **Save** button.
   b. In the **File name** text box, specify the desired name.
   c. On the **Common** toolbar, click the **Save** button.
4. If necessary, close the page.
   - Choose **File→Close.**
   - Or, on the tabbed file chooser, click the **Close** button to close the page.

You can use the **New Page** button in the **Folder List** task pane or on the **Web Site** tab to create a new page and specify a name for the web page.

Procedure Reference: Create a Layout Using Predefined Layouts

To create a layout using predefined layouts:

1. Open the desired web page.
2. Display the **Layout Tables** task pane.
   - Choose **Task Panes→Layout Tables.**
   - Or, choose **Tables→Layout Tables.**
3. In the **Layout Tables** task pane, in the **Table layout** section, select the desired type of layout.
4. If necessary, set the page margins.
   a. Open the **Advanced** tab of the **Page Properties** dialog box.

- In the **Layout Tables** task pane, in the **Table properties** section, click the **Set Page Margins** link.

- Or, choose **File→Properties,** and in the **Page Properties** dialog box, select the **Advanced** tab.

b. On the **Advanced** tab of the **Page Properties** dialog box, in the **Top margin, Left Margin, Bottom Margin,** and **Right Margin** text boxes, type the desired value and click **OK** to set the margins for the page.

 The values are specified in pixels.

5. If necessary, click at the top-left corner of the web page and on the quick tag selector bar, select <form#form1> and press **Delete.**

6. If necessary, on the **Common** toolbar, click the **Save** button.

Procedure Reference: Create a Layout Using the Layout Table Tools

To create a layout using the layout table tools:

1. Open the desired web page.

2. Display the **Layout Tables** task pane.

3. Insert a new table.

- In the **Layout Tables** task pane, in the **New tables and cells** section, click the **Insert Layout Table** link to create a layout table of the default size.

- In the **Layout Tables** task pane, in the **New tables and cells** section, select the **Draw Layout Table** option and then on the web page, click and drag it to the desired region to draw a table.

- Or, on the **Tables** toolbar, select the **Draw Layout Table** option and then on the web page, click and drag to draw a table of the desired size.

4. If desired, create a new cell in the table.

- Create a new cell in the table using the **Insert Layout Cell** link.

    a. In the **Layout Tables** task pane, in the **New tables and cells** section, click the **Insert Layout Cell** link.

    b. If necessary, in the **Insert Layout Cell** dialog box, in the **Layout** section, in the **Width** and **Height** text boxes, type the desired value.

    c. In the **Location** section, select the desired option to specify the placement of a cell with respect to the cell that has been added already.

- Select the **Draw Layout Cell** option and then in the table, click and drag to the desired region to draw a cell of the desired size and to create a new cell.

- Or, in the **Layout Tables** task pane, select the **Draw Layout Cell** option and then in the table, click and drag to the desired region to draw a cell of the desired size and to create a new cell.

5. If necessary, set the page margins.

6. If necessary, resize a cell using the layout tools.

7. If necessary, on the **Common** toolbar, click the **Save** button.

Procedure Reference: Customize a Layout Table Using the Table Properties Dialog Box

To customize a layout table using the **Table Properties** dialog box:

1. Open the desired web page that contains the table.
2. Open the **Table Properties** dialog box.
   - Right-click in the table and choose **Table Properties.**
   - Or, place the insertion point in the table and choose **Table→Table Properties→ Table.**
3. Customize the table settings.
   - In the **Size** section, specify the desired number of rows and columns.
   - In the **Layout** section, specify the layout settings.
   - In the **Borders** section, specify the border settings.
   - In the **Background** section, set the desired background for the table.
   - In the **Layout** section, check the **Enable layout tools** check box to view and work with the layout tools.
   - In the **Set** section, check the **Set as default for new tables** check box.
4. Click **Apply** and then click **OK.**
5. If necessary, on the **Common** toolbar, click the **Save** button.

Procedure Reference: Customize a Layout Table Using the Menu Options

To customize a layout table using the menu options:

1. Open the desired web page that contains the table.
2. Customize the table.
   - Merge the cells.
     a. Select a continuous row or column of cells.
        - Place the insertion point in a cell, press **Shift,** and click in the desired cell to select a series of cells.
        - Or, place the mouse pointer in a cell and click and drag to the desired cell.
     b. Merge the selected cells.
        - Choose **Table→Modify→Merge Cells.**
        - Right-click in the selected cell and choose **Modify→Merge Cells.**
        - Or, on the **Tables** toolbar, click **Merge Cells.**
   - Split a cell.
     a. Place the insertion point in a cell and open the **Split Cells** dialog box.
        - Choose **Table→Modify→Split Cells.**
        - Right-click in the cell and choose **Modify→Split Cells.**
        - Or, on the **Tables** toolbar, select the **Split Cells** option.
     b. In the **Split Cells** dialog box, select the required option.
        - Select the **Split into columns** option and click **OK.**

          Or, select the **Split into rows** option and click **OK.**

   c.   If necessary, in the **Number of columns** or **Number of rows** text box, type the required number of columns or rows, respectively, to split the cell into the desired number of rows or columns.

- Add cells.

   ■   Click inside the cell and choose **Table→Insert** and then select **Column to the Left, Column to the Right, Row Above, Row Below, Cell to the Left,** or **Cell to the Right** to add columns or rows to the table.

   ■   Or, click inside the cell and on the **Tables** toolbar, click **Column to the Left, Column to the Right, Row Above,** or **Row Below** to add columns or rows to the selected table.

- Delete cells.

   ■   Click inside the cell and choose **Table→Delete** and then choose the desired option to delete the selected cell.

   ■   Or, click inside the cell and on the **Tables** toolbar, click **Delete Cells.**

3.   If necessary, on the **Common** toolbar, click the **Save** button.

Procedure Reference: Add Background to a Web Page

To add background to a web page:

1.   Open the desired web page.
2.   Open the **Formatting** tab of the **Page Properties** dialog box.

- Choose **Format→Background.**
- Or, right-click the page and choose **Page Properties** and then in the **Page Properties** dialog box, select the **Formatting** tab.

3.   Add a background image.

   a.   In the **Page Properties** dialog box, on the **Formatting** tab, in the **Background** section, check the **Background picture** check box.

   b.   If necessary, check the **Make it a watermark** check box.

   c.   Click **Browse.**

   d.   In the **Select Background Picture** dialog box, navigate to the required folder, select the image, and click **Open.**

4.   If desired, add background color.

- In the **Page Properties** dialog box, in the **Colors** section, from the **Background** drop-down list, select the desired color.
- If necessary, from the **Background** drop-down list, select **More Colors** and then in the **More Colors** dialog box, choose desired options.

5.   In the **Page Properties** dialog box, click **OK.**
6.   If necessary, on the **Common** toolbar, click the **Save** button.
7.   If necessary, save the background image.

   a.   If desired, use the options in the **Save Embedded Files** dialog box.

   b.   In the **Save Embedded Files** dialog box, click **OK.**

Procedure Reference: Add Background to a Cell

To add background to a cell:

1.   Open the desired web page that contains the table.

2. Open the **Cell Properties** dialog box.

   - Right-click in the cell and choose **Cell Properties.**
   - Or, place the insertion point in the cell and choose **Table→Table Properties→Cell.**

3. In the **Cell Properties** dialog box, in the **Background** section, add the desired background color.

4. If necessary, add a background image.

5. In the **Cell Properties** dialog box, click **OK.**

6. If necessary, on the **Common** toolbar, click the **Save** button.

7. If necessary, save the background image in the desired location.

ACTIVITY 2-1

Designing a Layout Using Layout Tables

Before You Begin:

1. Close the **Tag properties, Toolbox,** and **Apply Styles** task pane groups.
2. Open your WSS site.

Scenario:

You are currently involved in a project that involves creating a subsite for the Human Resources department of Our Global Company. To start off with this project, your graphic designer has given you an image of the website layout. You want to replicate the same in SharePoint Designer using a layout table.

What You Do	How You Do It
1. Create a new subsite.	a. Choose **File→New→Web Site.**
	b. In the **New** dialog box, on the **Web Site** tab, in the left pane, select the **General** category.
	c. Verify that in the middle pane the **One Page Web Site** option is selected.
	d. In the **Specify the location of the new Web site** text box, click and type *http://[site name]/HumanResources*
	e. Click **OK.**

2. Create a layout table on a new web page.

a. Choose **File→New→ASPX.**

b. Choose **Task Panes→Layout Tables** to display the **Layout Tables** task pane.

c. Click the **Layout Tables** task pane title bar and drag it to the bottom of the editing window to dock it below the editing window.

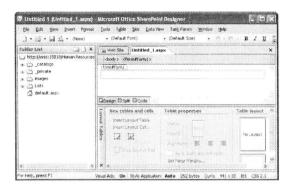

d. In the **Layout Tables** task pane, in the **Table layout** section, select the **Header, Footer, and 3 Columns** layout.

e. In the **Table properties** section, click the **Set Page Margins** link to open the **Page Properties** dialog box.

f. On the **Advanced** tab, in the **Top Margin** text box, type *0* and press **Tab** to set the **Top Margin** property to zero.

g. Similarly, set the **Left Margin, Bottom Margin,** and **Right Margin** to zero.

h. Click **OK.**

i. Close the **Layout Tables** task pane.

3. Modify the table layout.

a. On the **Untitled_1.aspx** page, right-click the table and choose **Table Properties.**

b. In the **Table Properties** dialog box, in the **Layout** section, from the **Alignment** drop-down list, select **Center.**

c. In the **Specify width** text box, double-click and type *1000* and click **OK.**

Handwritten notes:

Base root site URL has a limitation of 256 bytes.

eg:

http://ogc:20000/humanresources

is better than

http://ogc:20000/human resources.

because space will be replaced with "%20" (eg 3 bytes).

d. Place the mouse pointer at the bottom border of the footer cell and when it turns to a four-headed arrow, click to select the cell.

e. Press **Delete.**

f. Place the mouse pointer near the column width label of the table's bottom border and when it changes to a T shape, drag it upward until it touches the borders of the three columns.

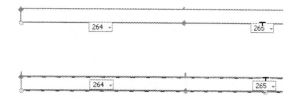

g. In the top border of the table, from the first column width label drop-down list, select **Change Column Width.**

h. In the **Column Properties** dialog box, in the **Column Width** text box, type *150* and click **OK.**

i. In the top border of the table, from the second column width label drop-down list, select **Change Column Width.**

j. In the **Column Properties** dialog box, in the **Column Width** text box, type *660* and click **OK.**

4. Add a background image to the **Untitled_1.aspx** page.

    a. Choose **Format→Background** to open the **Page Properties** dialog box.

    b. On the **Formatting** tab, in the **Background** section, check the **Background picture** check box and click **Browse.**

    c. In the **Select Background Picture** dialog box, navigate to the **C:\084721Data\ Creating a Subsite** folder.

    d. Select **background.JPG** and click **Open.**

    e. Check the **Make it a watermark** check box and click **OK.**

---

5. Add background color to the layout table's cell.

    a. Click the cell in the second row, second column and choose **Table→Table Properties→Cell.**

    b. In the **Cell Properties** dialog box, in the **Background** section, from the **Color** drop-down list, select the **White** color and click **OK.**

    c. Place the insertion point in the top-left corner of the **Untitled_1.aspx** page and then on the quick tag selector bar, select the **<form#form1>** tag, 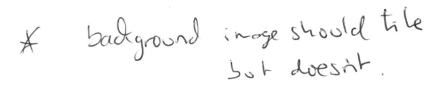 and press **Delete** to delete the form tag.

* background image should tile but doesn't.

TOPIC B

Create a Master Page

You have created a subsite and also designed the layout of a web page. To apply the same layout to all the web pages, you will need to save it as a template. In this topic, you will create a master page.

Trying to create the same type of layout for all your web pages manually can be time consuming. It would be easier if you can create the layout once and apply the same to all the web pages. With SharePoint Designer, you can save your layout page as a master page and apply the same layout to all the web pages in your site.

The Master Page

Definition:

The *master page* is an ASP.NET page that enables you to automatically display the standard elements of a website on all pages. Apart from the standard layout components such as the banners and navigation links, the master page has at least one content region tag where the editable content on each page will be added.

Example:

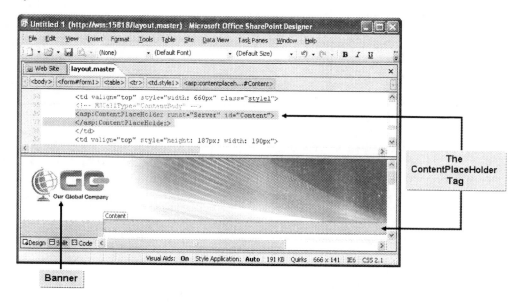

Standard Layout Components

Standard layout components are elements that you want to be displayed on all the pages of a website. Usually, elements such as the navigation links, the banner image, the logo and the footer text are standard elements present across all the pages of a website. These standard layout components can be added to the master page, which can be easily attached to any ASPX page using SharePoint Designer.

Content Regions

Definition:

A *content region* is a region that is defined on a master page. It facilitates the addition of content, which keeps changing with each page. Using content regions while designing websites ensures that the standard elements of a page remain unaltered while at the same time retaining the designer's freedom to work with page-specific content.

Example:

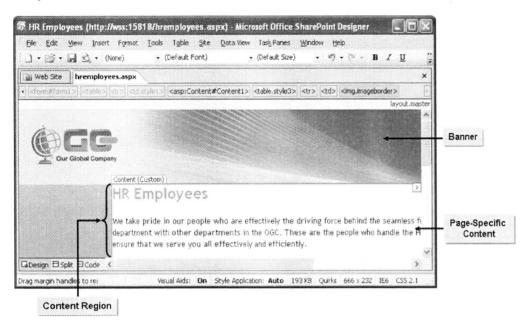

The Master Page Toolbar

The **Master Page** toolbar enables you to work with the content regions and also show or hide the labels of each content region on a master page. There are three options on the **Master Page** toolbar.

Figure 2-9: The components of the Master Page toolbar.

The following table lists the options on the **Master Page** toolbar.

Option	Enables You To
Regions	Select a specific content region from a listing of all content regions.
Manage Content Regions	Launch the **Manage Content Regions** dialog box using which you can add, delete, or rename content regions.
Template Region Labels	Toggle between the show and hide states of the content region names displayed as labels in the design view.

The Manage Content Regions Dialog Box

The **Manage Content Regions** dialog box enables you to manage content regions in an ASPX page.

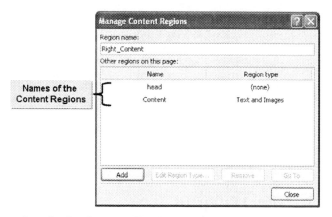

Figure 2-10: The options in the Content Region dialog box.

The following table lists the options in the **Manage Content Regions** dialog box.

Option	Enables You To
The **Region Name** text box	Specify a name to rename an existing name or to add a new region name.
The **Other regions on this page** section	List all the content regions on a master page. It also allows you to add and edit the region type of the selected content region.
The **Add, Rename** buttons	Add a new content region to the page or rename an existing region. The **Add** button becomes active once you specify a region name in the **Region Name** text box. When a region in the **Other regions on this page** section is double-clicked, the **Add** button changes to the **Rename** button. To add another content region, you need to close the dialog box and open it again.

Option	Enables You To
The **Edit Region Type** button	Edit the region type of the selected content region.
The **Remove** button	Remove an existing region from an ASPX page.
The **Go To** button	Navigate among the different content regions in a page.

The Save Embedded Files Dialog Box

The **Save Embedded Files** dialog box enables you to save files that are embedded on a web page. The **Embedded files to save** section displays the name of the files and the folder in which you want to save the file and the action that needs to be performed for each file. The **Picture preview** section allows you to preview a selected image. Using the buttons in this dialog box, you can rename a file, change the folder, set an action to save the file in the website folder or use the current file, and change the image file type.

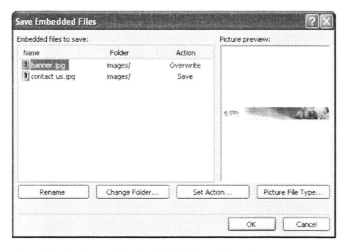

Figure 2-11: The options in the Save Embedded Files dialog box.

Context Menus

A *Context menu* is a menu that appears when you right-click specific elements in the application window. The options in the context menus differ based on the context in which they are accessed. They act as shortcut options to perform certain tasks because these options can also be accessed from the **Menu** bar. In SharePoint Designer, the context menu appears for elements such as toolbars and task panes.

 There are other application elements, such as the **Web Site** tab, scroll bars, tables, images, and the design view and code view, for which the context menu appears.

How to Create a Master Page

Procedure Reference: Add Images to a Web Page

To add images to a web page:

1. Open the **Picture** dialog box.
   - Choose **Insert→Picture→From File** to insert picture from the local computer.
   - Or, choose **Insert→Picture→From Scanner or Camera** to insert pictures from a scanner or camera.
2. In the **Picture** dialog box, navigate to the required folder.
3. Select the desired image and click **Insert.**
4. In the **Accessibility Properties** dialog box, in the **Alternate text** text box, type an alternate text for the image.
5. If necessary, click **Browse** and then in the **Select Long Description** dialog box, navigate to the required folder and open the file.

Procedure Reference: Save an ASPX Page as a Master Page

To save an ASPX page as a master page:

1. Open the ASPX page with the layout of the website.
2. Choose **File→Save As.**
3. Change the extension of the web page to master.
   - In the **Save As** dialog box, from the **Save as type** drop-down list, select **Master Page (*.master).**
   - Or, in the **File name** text box, type the file name with a **master** extension.
4. Click **Save.**
5. In the **Microsoft Office SharePoint Designer** message box, click **Yes.**

Procedure Reference: Create Content Regions on a Master Page

To create content regions on a master page:

1. Open a master or an ASPX page.
2. Place the insertion pointer on the web page as desired.
3. Display the **Manage Content Regions** dialog box.
   - Choose **Format→Master Page→Manage Content Regions.**
   - Or, on the **Master Page** toolbar, click the **Manage Content Regions** button.
4. In the **Manage Content Regions** dialog box, in the **Region name** text box, type the name of the content region.
5. Click **Add** to create a content region and then click **Close.**
6. If desired, on the quick tag selector bar, select the **<p>** tag and press **Delete** to remove the **<p>** tag from the content region.

 When you specify a content region on an ASPX page, the extension automatically becomes .master.

7. Save the page.

Removing the <p> Tag from the Content Region

Content regions are defined on the master page. While specifying a name for a content region in the **Manage Content Regions** dialog box, SharePoint Designer creates a **<p>** tag with the region name in the master page's content region. When the master page is linked to web pages, the **<p>** tag along with the region name, will be displayed on all the pages. You will have to manually delete the **<p>** tags before adding new content to the pages as an extra white space appears above the content area when viewed on other browsers such as Netscape Navigator.

ACTIVITY 2-2

Creating a Master Page

Scenario:

As you progress with the development of the website, you want to make the layout available for all the pages on the site. You will therefore add the standard layout components to the layout, create the content regions, and save it as a master page.

What You Do	How You Do It
1. Add the standard images to the layout.	a. On the **Untitled_1.aspx** page, in the header section of the layout table, click and choose **Insert→Picture→From File.**

 The header section is the first row in a layout table.

	b. In the **Picture** dialog box, navigate to the **C:\084721Data\Creating a Subsite** folder.
	c. Select the **banner1.JPG** image and click **Insert.**
	d. In the **Accessibility Properties** dialog box, in the **Alternate text** text box, type *Our Global Company* and click **OK.**
	e. Place the insertion point in the second row, third column and choose **Insert→Picture→From File.**
	f. In the **Picture** dialog box, open the **contact us.JPG** image. Set the text *Contact Us* as the alternate text.

2.	Define a content region.	a.	Choose **View→Toolbars→Master Page.**
		b.	If necessary, reposition the **Master Page** toolbar to the desired location.
		c.	Place the insertion point in the second row, second column and on the **Master Page** toolbar, click **Manage Content Regions.**
		d.	If necessary, in the **Microsoft Office SharePoint Designer** message box, click **Yes.**
		e.	In the **Manage Content Regions** dialog box, in the **Region name** text box, type *Content* and click **Add.**
		f.	Click **Close.**
		g.	On the quick tag selector bar, select the **<p>** tag, and press **Delete** to delete the para tag.
		h.	Close the **Master Page** toolbar.
3.	Save the page as a master page.	a.	On the **Common** toolbar, click **Save.**
		b.	In the **Save As** dialog box, verify that the address is **http://[site name]/ HumanResources.**
		c.	In the **File name** text box, type *layout*
		d.	From the **Save as type** drop-down list, select **Master Page** and click **Save.**
		e.	In the **Microsoft Office SharePoint Designer** message box, click **Yes** twice.
		f.	In the **Save Embedded Files** dialog box, click **Change Folder.**
		g.	In the **Change Folder** dialog box, select the **images** folder and click **OK.**
		h.	In the **Save Embedded Files** dialog box, click **OK.**
		i.	Close **layout.master.**

TOPIC C
Modify a Page Layout

You have created a subsite and designed the layout for the site. There may be times when you would want to modify the layout to suit a specific need. In this topic, you will modify the layout of a web page.

Sometimes you might not be satisfied with the default layout, or with the layout that you created. You might want to edit the layout to suit your requirements. SharePoint Designer provides you with an easy-to-use tool and options that helps you to modify the layouts.

The Select a Master Page Dialog Box

The **Select a Master Page** dialog box contains options that enable you to specify the master page that you want to attach to a web page.

Figure 2-12: *The options in the Select a Master Page dialog box.*

The following table lists the options in the **Select a Master Page** dialog box.

Option	Enables You To
Default Master Page (~Masterurl.default.master)	Link the web page to the default master page.
Custom Master Page (~Masterurl.custom.master)	Link the web page to the customized master page.
Specific Master Page	Browse to a specific location and select the master page to which you want to link the web page.

Default Page Customization

SharePoint Designer allows you to customize the default master page (default.master) and the CSS stylesheet (core.css) in a SharePoint site. When the default master page/stylesheet in a SharePoint site is modified, a blue icon appears beside the master page/stylesheet icon. If you are not satisfied with the customization you have made, the *safety net feature* of SharePoint Designer allows you to revert to the default scheme by right-clicking the master page icon and choosing **Reset to Site Definition.** When this is done, a copy of the customized page will also be created and saved onto the SharePoint site.

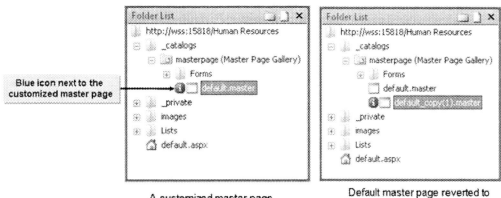

Blue icon next to the customized master page

A customized master page

Default master page reverted to its original state and a copy of the customized master page

The Preview in Browser Option

The **Preview in Browser** option allows you to preview a web page in a browser. You can select the browser type, browser version, and the size of the browser window in which you want to preview the web page. You can add or modify the browser list using the **Edit Browser List** dialog box.

The Edit Browser List Dialog Box

The **Edit Browser List** dialog box enables you to add and modify the browser list. It contains the **Browsers** section, which lists the names of the browsers that are installed in your system. You can choose the browsers that you want to be launched while previewing in multiple browsers in the **Use the check boxes in the list to select the group of browsers that will be launched when using "Preview in Multiple Browsers"** list box. It also contains options that enable you to add, modify, and remove browsers from the list. The **Additional window sizes** section enables you to choose the size of the browser window. The **Automatically save page before previewing** check box enables you to automatically save the page once you click the **Preview in Browser** button. It can accessed by choosing **File→Preview in Browser→Edit Browser list.**

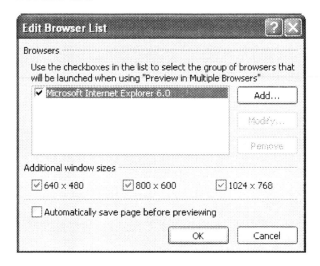

How to Modify the Master Page Layout

Procedure Reference: Modify the Master Page Layout

To modify the master page layout:

1. Open the page containing the layout that needs to be edited.
2. Editing the layout of the web page.
   - Merge the necessary cells.
   - Split the desired cells.
   - Delete the unused images and the content regions.
   - Add images to the web page.
   - Resize the cells using the layout tools or the **Cell Properties** dialog box.
3. Save the page.

Procedure Reference: Link a Web Page to a Master Page

To link a web page to a master page:

1. Open a web page.
   - Create a new ASPX page.
   - Or, open an existing web page.
     - In the **Folder List** task pane, double-click the desired file.
     - Or, on the **Web Site** tab, double-click the desired file.
2. Choose **Format→Master Page→Attach Master Page.**
3. In the **Select a Master Page** dialog box, specify the master page that needs to be attached to the web page.

 When a master page is attached to an existing web page, SharePoint Designer matches content on the web page with a content region on the master page using the **Match Content Regions** dialog box.

4. If desired, add content to the content region of the web page that is linked to the master page.
   a. Select the content region, click the right arrow beside the region, and click **Create Custom Content.**
   b. In the content region, add the necessary graphic or text.
5. If necessary, save the page.

Procedure Reference: Preview a Web Page in a Browser

To preview a web page in a browser:

1. Open a web page in SharePoint Designer.

2. Preview the page.

- Choose **File→Preview in Browser** and choose the required browser option in which you want to preview.
- Click the **Preview in Browser** button to preview the page in the default browser.
- Or, from the **Preview in Browser** drop-down list, select the required browser option in which you want to preview.

3. If necessary, close the browser window.

ACTIVITY 2-3
Modifying the Layout of a Master Page

Scenario:
You've designed a new layout for the subsite. You realize that you need to attach some of the web pages to the default master page available in the subsite. As the default master page does not contain the banner image and has several unnecessary cells and elements that hinder the placement of the banner image, you decide to modify the layout of the master page and link it to a web page.

What You Do	How You Do It
1. Open the **default.master** page.	a. In the **Folder List** task pane, expand the **_catalogs** folder to display the contents of the folder.
	b. Expand the **masterpage (Master Page Gallery)** folder and then double-click the **default.master** page to open the page.
2. Modify the layout.	a. On the **default.master** page, in the top-right corner, select the search control and press **Delete.**
	b. Select the image at the top-left corner and press **Delete.**

c. Hold down **Shift** and click in the extreme right of the cell.

d. Right-click in the selected table and choose **Modify→Merge Cells** to merge the selected cells.

e. Click in the first content region of the selected cell and then press the **Left Arrow** key three times to place the insertion point outside the content region.

✳ Dont do these Recommendations. ✳

3. Add the banner image to the subsite and the top-level site.

    a. Open the **Picture** dialog box.

    b. In the **Picture** dialog box, open the **banner2.JPG** image and set the text *Our Global Company* as the alternate text.

    c. On the **Common** toolbar, click the **Save** button.

    d. In the **Site Definition Page Warning** message box, click **Yes.**

    e. In the **Save Embedded Files** dialog box, verify that the **images** folder is listed and click **OK.**

    f. Maximize the top-level site.

    g. From the **Folder List** task pane, open the master page of the top-level site.

    h. On the master page, delete the search control, text, and image and then merge the cells.

    i. Press the **Left Arrow** key and then from the **C:\084721Data\Creating a Subsite** folder, insert the **banner2.JPG** image with **Our Global Company** as the alternate text. Save the master page and the image in the **images** folder.

    j. Choose **File→Exit** to close the application.

4. Attach the master page to the **default.aspx** page.

    a. In the **Folder List** task pane, double-click the **default.aspx** page to open it.

    b. Choose **Format→Master Page→Attach Master Page.**

    c. In the **Select a Master Page** dialog box, verify that the **Default Master Page (~masterurl/default.master)** option is selected and click **OK.**

    d. Save default.aspx.

    e. On the **Common** toolbar, click the **Preview in Browser** button, to preview the page in the browser.

    f. Close the browser window.

    g. Close the **default.aspx** and the **default.master** pages.

Lesson 2 Follow-up

In this lesson, you created a subsite by defining the layout and content regions. You also saved the layout page as a master page. This will enable you to have a consistent layout throughout the pages of your website.

1. **What do you think are the advantages of creating a layout using layout tables? Why?**

2. **Discuss the different types of layouts that can be created using SharePoint Designer and evaluate their advantages and disadvantages.**

3. **What do you think are the benefits of creating master pages?**

3 | Adding Content to the Site

Lesson Time: 1 hour(s)

Lesson Objectives:

In this lesson, you will add content to a web page.

You will:

- Add and format text.
- Work with tables.
- Work with images.

Introduction

You have created the layout for the site and are all set to create the web pages. The first thing you would probably do after defining the layout is to get started with adding content to the web pages. In this lesson, you will add content to the web pages.

All websites exist to provide information in some form to a specific audience. It is imperative that the content you add to a website be relevant and more importantly, the content should be presented in such a manner that it holds the interest of the visitors to your site. Using SharePoint Designer, you can easily populate your web pages with text, tables, and images, and also format them, thereby enhancing the presentation elements of your website content.

TOPIC A
Add and Format Text

You have created the master page of the website. The next step would be to get started with building the website by adding the required web pages and content. In this topic, you will add text to a web page and format it.

It is a tedious process if you have to type out the text for a number of web pages. You can save a lot of time and effort if you can import files into your website or copy text from the source file to the web page directly. Also, textual content in its default format looks unappealing and may not be readable. SharePoint Designer allows you to add text from a wide range of text editors and word processors and also format it in the desired manner.

The Paste Text Dialog Box

The **Paste Text** dialog box contains options that allow you to paste text that is copied from other applications.

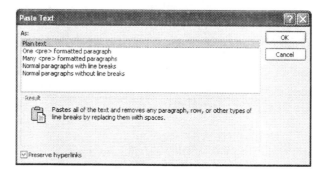

Figure 3-1: *The options in the Paste Text dialog box.*

The following table describes the options in the **Paste Text** dialog box.

Option	Description
Plain Text	Pastes all text but replaces line breaks with spaces.
One \<pre\> formatted paragraph	Pastes all text within a single preformatted text \<pre\> tag.
Many \<pre\> formatted paragraphs	Pastes each paragraph into separate \<pre\> tags.
Normal paragraphs with line breaks	Pastes all text within a single paragraph tag.
Normal paragraphs without line breaks	Pastes each paragraph into a separate paragraph tag.

Paste vs. Paste Text

Applications such as Microsoft Word use style sheets and markup languages to format text. The **Paste** option copies text along with the markup and styles, thereby increasing the file size. SharePoint Designer helps you to overcome this challenge with the **Paste Text** option that launches the **Paste Text** dialog box, which allows you to have more control over how the text should be copied and pasted. The **Paste Text** dialog box ensures that the markup and styles accompanying the text are not copied.

The Import Dialog Box

The *Import dialog box* enables you to add files and even entire folders to the website folder. You can also import files from a remote server. In addition to enabling these functions, the **Import** dialog box allows you to modify the URL of a file and remove added files from the import list.

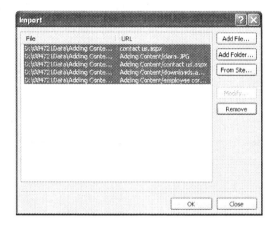

Figure 3-2: The options in the Import dialog box.

The Spelling Dialog Box

The **Spelling** dialog box provides you with options to spell check a web page.

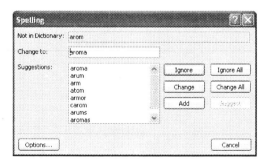

Figure 3-3: The options in the Spelling dialog box.

The following table lists the options in the **Spelling** dialog box.

Option	Enables You To
Ignore	Ignore the current misspelled word.
Ignore All	Ignore all the words that are similarly misspelled.
Change	Change the word to the selected suggestion.
Change All	Change all the words that are similarly misspelled and repeated on the web page.
Add	Add the misspelled word to the list of words in the dictionary.
Suggest	List a set of suggestions for the word you type in the **Change To** text box.
Options	Display the **Spelling Options** dialog box to customize the spelling options such as flagging repeated words and hiding spelling errors.

The Formatting Toolbar

The *Formatting toolbar* contains options to change the font type, size, and other basic text properties. Apart from the standard formatting options, the **Formatting** toolbar provides two unique formatting options—**Manage Styles** and **Style.** The **Manage Styles** option helps you to launch the **Manage Styles** task pane with just a click of a button and the **Style** drop-down list allows you to change the HTML tags from the design view. Most of the options on the **Formatting** toolbar are also available on the **Common** toolbar.

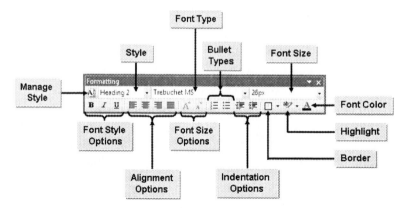

Figure 3-4: The options on the Formatting toolbar.

How to Add and Format Text

Procedure Reference: Add a Title to a Web Page

To add a title to a web page:

1. Open the desired web page.
2. Display the **Page Properties** dialog box.
   - Right-click on the page and choose **Page Properties.**
   - Or, choose **File→Properties.**
3. In the **Page Properties** dialog box, on the **General** tab, in the **Title** text box, type the desired title for the page.
4. Click **OK.**
5. Save the web page.
6. On the **Common** toolbar, click the **Preview in Browser** button to view the title in the title bar of the browser window.

Procedure Reference: Rename a Web Page

To rename a web page:

1. Open the desired web page.
2. Choose the **Rename** option.
   - In the **Web Site** pane, right-click the name of the desired web page and choose **Rename.**
   - Or, in the **Folder List** pane, right-click the name of the desired web page and choose **Rename.**
3. Type the required name and press **Enter.**

 Ensure that you type the name with its appropriate file extension.

4. If necessary, in the **Confirm Rename** dialog box, check the **Don't show me again** check box.
5. Click **Yes.**

Procedure Reference: Copy Text to a Web Page

To copy text to a web page:

1. Open the file containing the required text.
2. Select the required text.
3. Copy the content.
   - Choose **Edit→Copy.**
   - Or, press **Ctrl+C.**
4. Create a new page or open the desired web page in SharePoint Designer.
5. If necessary, link the web page to the master page.
6. Transfer text.
   - Paste the content.

- Choose **Edit→Paste.**
- Press **Ctrl+V.**
- Or, on the **Standard** toolbar, click the **Paste** button.
- Or, paste the content using the **Paste Text** dialog box.
    a. Choose **Edit→Paste Text.**
    b. In the **Paste Text** dialog box, in the **As** list box, select the desired option.
    c. Click **OK.**

7. Save and preview the page.

Procedure Reference: Import Web Pages to a Website

To import web pages to a website:

1. Choose **File→Import→File.**
2. In the **Import** dialog box, click the desired button.
   - Click **Add File** to add a file to the site.
   - Click **Add Folder** to add a folder to the site.
   - Click **From Site** to add a file from a remote server.
3. If necessary, from the **File** list, select a file or folder and click **Remove** to remove a file from the list.
4. If necessary, from the **File** list, select a file or folder and click **Modify** to change the path of a file in the list.
5. In the **Import** dialog box, click **OK.**
6. If necessary, move the added file to the desired folder using the **Folder List** task pane.
   - Drag the file to the desired folder.
   - Or, cut the file and paste it into the desired folder.

Procedure Reference: Import Content from an External File to a Web Page

To import content from an external file to a web page:

1. Create a new ASPX page or open an existing page.
2. Choose **Insert→File.**
3. In the **Select File** dialog box, navigate to the desired file and click **Open** to import the content of the file onto the web page.

   The commonly used file types are HTML Files (*.htm, *.html), Rich Text Format (*.rtf), Text (*.txt), Word 2007 Document (*.docx), and Word 97–2003 Document (*.doc).
4. Save and preview the page.

Procedure Reference: Format Text

To format text on a web page:

1. Open the desired web page.
2. Select the desired text.
3. Choose **View→Toolbars→Formatting** to display the Formatting toolbar.

4. Format the text.

- Format the text using the font options: **Font, Font Size, Increase Font Size,** and **Decrease Font Size.**

- Format the text by changing the style options: **Style, Bold, Italic, Underline,** and **Outside Border.**

- Format the text by using the list options: **Numbering** and **Bullets.**

- Format the text by using the aligning options: **Align Text Left, Center, Align Text Right, Justify, Decrease Indent Position,** and **Increase Indent Position.**

- Format the text by using the color options: **Highlight** and **Font Color.**

5. Save and preview the page.

Procedure Reference: Spell Check a Web Page

To spell check a web page:

1. Open the desired web page.
2. Spell check the page.

   - Choose **Tools→Spelling→Spelling.**
   - Or, press **F7.**

3. In the **Spelling** dialog box, choose the appropriate option to correct the misspelled word.
4. In the **Microsoft Office SharePoint Designer** message box, click **OK.**
5. Save and preview the page.

ACTIVITY 3-1

Adding Text to a Web Page

Scenario:

You have a document that contains the latest news releases about your organization. You want to present this information within the web page layout that you have designed. You would like to transfer the information from the document to the web page.

What You Do	How You Do It
1. Attach the master page to a new page.	a. In the **Folder List** task pane, select the root folder.
	b. Choose **File→New→ASPX**.
	c. Choose **Format→Master Page→Attach Master Page**.
	d. In the **Select a Master Page** dialog box, select the **Specific Master Page** option and click **Browse**.
	e. In the **Select a Master Page** dialog box, in the left pane, select **Current Site**.
	f. Select **layout.master** and click **Open**.
	g. In the **Select a Master Page** dialog box, click **OK**.
2. Add a title to the page.	a. Choose **File→Properties**.
	b. In the **Page Properties** dialog box, on the **General** tab, in the **Title** text box, type *Our Global Company* and click **OK**.

3.	Open a Word document.	a.	Choose **Start→All Programs→Microsoft Office→Microsoft Office Word 2007.**
		b.	If necessary, in the **Welcome to the 2007 Microsoft Office System** dialog box, click **Next,** select the **I don't want to use Microsoft updates** option, and click **Finish.**
		c.	Click **Office Button** and choose **Open.**
		d.	Navigate to the **C:\084721Data\Adding Content** folder.
		e.	Select **news release.doc** and click **Open.**

4.	Transfer the content of the Word document to the web page.	a.	On the **Home** tab, in the **Editing** group, click **Select** and select **Select All.**

		b.	In the **Clipboard** group, click **Copy** to copy the text.

		c.	Close Microsoft Word.
		d.	On the **Untitled_1.aspx** page, click the content region, click the right arrow beside the **Content(Master)** region, and click **Create Custom Content.**

e. Click on the blank area below **Content(Custom)** and choose **Edit→ Paste Text.**

f. In the **Paste Text** dialog box, in the **As** list box, select **Normal paragraphs without line breaks.**

g. Click **OK** to paste the text.

---

5. Save and preview the page.

    a. Click the **Save** button.

    b. In the **Save As** dialog box, in the **File name** text box, type *newsrelease* and click **Save.**

    c. Click the **Preview in Browser** button to preview the page.

    d. Close the browser window.

ACTIVITY 3-2

Importing Web Pages to a Website

Data Files:

employeecorner.aspx, clara.JPG, finance team1.JPG

Scenario:

Your team members are helping you create some of the web pages needed for your subsite. Once your team members complete developing the individual.aspx pages, they send it to you for integrating them onto the subsite.

What You Do	How You Do It
1. Add a web page to the website.	a. Choose **File→Import→File.**
	b. In the **Import** dialog box, click **Add File.**
	c. In the **Add File to Import List** dialog box, navigate to the **C:\084721Data\Adding Content** folder.
	d. Select **employeecorner.aspx** and ctrl-click **clara.JPG** and **finance team1.JPG.**

 When a web page is imported, the images contained on the web page should also be imported. If the images are not imported, empty image placeholders are displayed on the web page.

	e. Click **Open** to add the web page and the images to the import list.
	f. In the **Import** dialog box, click **OK.**

2.	Attach the master page to the employee corner page.	a.	In the **Folder List** task pane, double-click **employeecorner.aspx.**
		b.	Choose **Format→Master Page→Attach Master Page.**
		c.	In the **Select a Master Page** dialog box, select the **Specific Master Page** option, and click **Browse.**
		d.	In the **Select a Master Page** dialog box, in the left pane, select **Current Site.**
		e.	Select **layout.master** and click **Open.**
		f.	In the **Select a Master Page** dialog box, click **OK.**
		g.	In the **Match Content Regions** dialog box, click **OK.**
3.	Move the images to the **Images** folder.	a.	In the **Folder List** task pane, select **clara.JPG** and ctrl-click **finance team1.JPG.**
		b.	Drag the selected images to the **Images** folder.
4.	Spell check the employee corner page.	a.	Click anywhere on the web page.
		b.	Choose **Tools→Spelling→Spelling.**
		c.	Observe that the misspelled word "distiction" is displayed in the **Not in Dictionary** text box and the correct word "distinction" is displayed in the **Change to** text box of the **Spelling** dialog box.
		d.	In the **Spelling** dialog box, click **Change** to change the misspelled word.
		e.	In the **Microsoft Office SharePoint Designer** message box, click **OK.**

5.	Save and preview the employee corner page.	**a.** Click the **Save** button.
		b. If necessary, in the **Confirm Save** message box, click **Yes.**
		c. Click the **Preview in Browser** button.
		d. Close the browser window.
		e. Close employeecorner.aspx.

ACTIVITY 3-3
Formatting Text

Before You Begin:
On the **newsrelease.aspx** page, scroll to the top of the page.

Scenario:
You notice that the text that is presented on the News Release page looks visually unappealing and monotonous. So, you decide to make the text look more visually appealing and readable. You also want to highlight, underline, and change the color of the important text and make critical information stand out from the rest of the content.

What You Do	How You Do It
1. Change the style of the header text.	a. Choose **View→Toolbars→Formatting**.
	b. If necessary, reposition the toolbar to the desired location.
	c. Click before the "News Release" text.
	d. On the **Formatting** toolbar, from the **Style** drop-down list, select **Heading 2 <h2>**.
	e. Observe that the text "News Release" has been formatted as heading 2 text.
	f. Change the style of the words "News" and "Events" to **Heading 3<h3>**.
	g. Change the style of the sub-headings below the "News" and "Events" headings to **Heading 4<h4>**.
2. Format the text using the **Bold** and **Underline** options.	a. Scroll up, and below the header "News Release", click before the text "Our Global" and shift-click after the text "their management".
	b. On the **Formatting** toolbar, click the **Bold** and **Underline** buttons.

3.	Change the color of the font.	a.	Scroll down, and select the text "August 12th".
		b.	On the **Formatting** toolbar, click the **Font Color** drop-down list.
		c.	Select **More Colors,** triple-click in the value text box, and type *6699FF*
		d.	Click **OK.**
		e.	Change the color of the text "December 14th" and "July 30th" to **6699FF.**
		f.	Close the **Formatting** toolbar.
4.	Save and preview the page.	a.	Click the **Save** button.
		b.	Click the **Preview in Browser** button.
		c.	Close the browser window.
		d.	Close newsrelease.aspx.

TOPIC B
Work with Tables

You added text to the web pages and formatted them. Some content may be more effective when they are presented in tables. In this topic, you will work with tables.

Many types of content such as financial information, comparative data, and lists can be much more clearly read and understood when it is presented in the form of a table. The same content when presented as text might become very lengthy and vague. SharePoint Designer allows you to add tables to your web pages and present complex information in a simple manner.

How to Work with Tables

Procedure Reference: Create a Table

To create a table:

1.   Open the desired web page.
2.   Choose **Table→Insert Table.**
3.   In the **Insert Table** dialog box, in the **Size** section, specify the number of rows and columns.
4.   Click **OK** to create a table.
5.   If necessary, format the table.
6.   Save and preview the page.

 The **Insert Table** dialog box is displayed whenever a table is created. But when you want to modify the table, the **Insert Table** dialog box changes to the **Table Properties** dialog box. Both the dialog boxes have the same set of options.

The Table AutoFormat Dialog Box

The **Table AutoFormat** dialog box allows you to format tables using predefined formatting options. This dialog box provides an extensive list of table designs, which you can apply to the tables you create. The **Table AutoFormat** dialog box can be accessed by choosing **Table→ Modify→Table AutoFormat** or right-clicking the table and choosing **Modify→Table AutoFormat.**

Procedure Reference: Format a Table

To format a table using the **Table Properties** dialog box:

1.   Open the desired web page.
2.   Select the desired table.
3.   Open the **Table Properties** dialog box.
     ●   Right-click in the table and choose **Table Properties.**
     ●   Or, place the insertion point in the table and choose **Table→Table Properties→ Table.**
4.   In the **Table Properties** dialog box, specify the desired settings to customize the table settings.

5. Click **Apply** and click **OK.**

6. If necessary, on the **Common** toolbar, click the **Save** button.

7. If necessary, on the **Common** toolbar, click the **Preview in Browser** button to view the web page.

ACTIVITY 3-4
Working with Tables

Data Files:

suggestedreading.aspx, contactus.aspx, downloads.aspx, termsandconditions.aspx, hremployees.aspx, steve.aspx, financeteam.aspx, finance team2.JPG, steve2.JPG, susan1.JPG, maria1.JPG, caroll.JPG, linda1.JPG

Before You Begin:

1. Open the suggested reading.doc file from the **C:\084721Data\Adding Content** folder.

2. Import the **suggestedreading.aspx, contactus.aspx, downloads.aspx, termsandconditions.aspx, hremployees.aspx, steve.aspx, financeteam.aspx** pages and the finance team2.JPG, steve2.JPG, susan1.JPG, maria1.JPG, caroll.JPG, linda1.JPG images to the Human Resources subsite.

3. Attach the **layout.master** page to the **suggestedreading.aspx, contactus.aspx, downloads.aspx, termsandconditions.aspx, steve.aspx,** and **financeteam.aspx** pages.

4. Move all the images to the **images** folder.

Scenario:

For the Human Resources subsite, you plan to add a web page that lists some of the popular books on human resource management. One of your colleagues suggests that it would look better if the information is presented in a tabular format.

What You Do	How You Do It
1. Create a table.	a. In the **Folder List** task pane, double-click **suggestedreading.aspx.**
	b. In the editing window, click after the word "reading." and choose **Table→Insert Table.**
	c. In the **Size** section, in the **Rows** spin box, type *6*
	d. On the keyboard, press **tab,** and in the **Columns** spin box, type *3* and click **OK.**

2. Add content to the table cells.	a. Switch to the suggested reading.doc file.
	b. From the suggested reading.doc file, copy the text "Book Name" and minimize the window.
	c. Restore the **suggestedreading.aspx** page.
	d. In the first row, in the first column, choose **Edit→Paste.**
	e. Copy paste content for the rest of the table from suggested reading.doc.

Book Name	Author Name	Book ID
People Management	Robert Davis	#987659
Payroll	Susan Baker	#765687
Employee Welfare	Jennifer Nelson	#668547
Leadership and Development	Barbara Green	#866879
Employee Retention	Steven Thompson	#76785

3. Apply borders to the table.	a. Right-click the table and choose **Table Properties.**
	b. In the **Table Properties** dialog box, in the **Borders** section, triple-click the **Size** spin box and type *1*
	c. In the **Borders** section, from the **Color** drop-down list, select **More Colors.**
	d. In the **More Colors** dialog box, in the **Value** text box, double-click and type *000080* and click **OK** to set blue as the new color.
	e. In the **Table Properties** dialog box, click **OK.**
4. Format the header row of the table.	a. In the left corner of the first row, when the pointer changes to a right arrow near the cell border, click the first row to select it.
	b. On the **Common** toolbar, from the **Style** drop-down list, select **Heading 3 <h3>.**
	c. On the **Common** toolbar, select the **Center** option.

5. Apply borders to the table cells.

    a. Click before the text "Book Name" and shift-click after the text "#76785" in the last cell.

Book Name	Author Name	Book ID
People Management	Robert Davis	#987659
Payroll	Susan Baker	#765687
Employee Welfare	Jennifer Nelson	#668547
Leadership and Development	Barbara Green	#668379
Employee Retention	Steven Thompson	#767855

    b. Choose **Table→Table Properties→Cell.**

    c. In the **Cell Properties** dialog box, in the **Borders** section, click the **Size** spin box and type *1*

    d. In the **Borders** section, from the **Color** drop-down list, in the **Document Colors** section, click the color **Navy.**

    e. Click **OK.**

6. Change the **Cell Padding** properties.

    a. Right-click the table and choose **Table Properties.**

    b. In the **Table Properties** dialog box, in the **Layout** section, double-click the **Cell padding** spin box and type *2*

7. Fix the borders of the table.

    a. In the **Layout** section, under the **Specify width** check box, double-click and type *600*

    b. Select the **In pixels** option and click **OK.**

8. Save and preview the page.

    a. Click the **Save** button.

    b. Click the **Preview in Browser** button.

    c. Observe the formatted table and close the browser window.

    d. Close suggestedreading.aspx.

    e. Close suggested reading.doc.

ACTIVITY 3-5

Managing Content Using Tables

Before You Begin:

From the **C:\084721Data\Adding Content** folder, open the home.doc file and minimize it.

Scenario:

To enhance the look and feel of the home page of the Human Resources subsite, you plan to populate it by adding some introductory text and the photo of the HR manager.

What You Do	How You Do It
1. Create a table.	a. In the **Folder List** task pane, double-click **default.aspx**.
	b. In the editing window click in the first content region, click the right arrow next to it, and choose **Create Custom Content**.

	c. Click inside the **PlaceHolderPageDescription (Custom)** content region.
	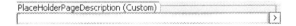
	d. Choose **Table→Insert Table.**
	e. In the **Size** section, in the **Rows** spin box, type *1*
	f. In the **Insert Table** dialog box, click **OK.**
2. Transfer the content from the home.doc file to the table cell.	a. Switch to the home.doc file.
	b. From the home.doc file, copy the entire text and close the window.
	c. Restore the **default.aspx** page.
	d. Choose **Edit→Paste.**

3. Add an image to the table cell.

    a. In the editing window, scroll to the right and click inside the second cell of the table.

    b. Choose **Insert→Picture→From File.**

    c. In the **Picture** dialog box, navigate to the **images** folder.

    d. Select the **carol1.JPG** image and click **Open.**

    e. In the **Accessibility Properties** dialog box, in the **Alternate text** text box, type *Carol* and click **OK.**

4. Save and preview the page.

    a. Click the **Save** button.

    b. Click the **Preview in Browser** button.

    c. Close the browser window.

    d. Close default.aspx.

TOPIC C
Work with Images

You are now familiar with creating tables and formatting them and you have also added an image to the master page. There may be times when you want to change or edit an image. In this topic, you will work with the images on your web pages.

Images form an integral part of any website. And, when building a website, there will be occasions where you will need to make some minor edits or modify some of these images. Instead of editing the images using a separate image editing software, SharePoint Designer provides you with image editing tools that enable you to edit these images.

The Pictures Toolbar

The *Pictures toolbar* contains several options that enable you to modify an image in a file.

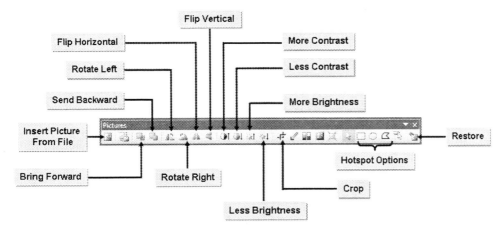

Figure 3-5: *The options on the Pictures toolbar.*

The following table lists the important options on the **Pictures** toolbar.

Option	Enables You To
The **Insert Picture From File** option	Add a new picture to the current web page from your local hard disk.
The **Bring Forward** and **Send Backward** options	Adjust the position of images on the page, relative to the position of other elements on the same page.
The **Rotate Left** and **Rotate Right** options	Rotate the selected image by 90 degrees to the left or right.
The **Flip Horizontal** and **Flip Vertical** options	Flip the selected image along its horizontal or vertical edge.
The **More Contrast** and **Less Contrast** options	Increase or decrease the amount of contrast in the selected image.
The **More Brightness** and **Less Brightness** options	Lighten or darken the selected image.

Option	Enables You To
The **Crop** option	Select a region of the image while deleting the remainder of the image.
The **Hotspot** options	Draw hotspots for linking an image.
The **Restore** option	Return an image to its original state.

Other Options on the Pictures Toolbar

The other options on the **Pictures** toolbar are as follows:

- The **Auto Thumbnail** option: Allows you to create a thumbnail image from the selected image.

- The **Set Transparent Color** option: Allows you to select a color from an image that will be transparent when displayed in a browser.

- The **Color** option: Allows you to set the color scheme for the selected image. Options are **Automatic, Grayscale, Black And White,** and **Washout.**

- The **Bevel** option: Allows you to add a beveled border to an image.

- The **Resample** option: Allows you to redraw an image according to its new size.

- The **Select** option: Allows you to select image components.

- The **Highlight Hotspots** option: Allows you to highlight the hotspot of the image.

The Tag Properties Task Pane

The **Tag Properties** task pane is a context-sensitive task pane that consists of various properties grouped under categories that are unique to the selected element of a web page. These categories vary based on whether the selected tag is an HTML tag or an ASPX tag. Some of the categories unique to ASP.NET controls include **Behavior, Data,** and **Misc.** The four buttons at the top of the **Tag Properties** task pane allow you to change the way the properties are listed.

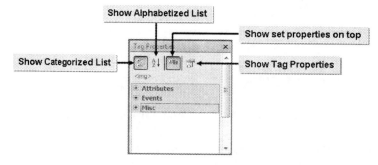

Figure 3-6: The options in the Tag Properties task pane.

Categories in the Tag Properties Task Pane for an ASPX Control

When an ASPX control is selected, the **Tag Properties** task pane displays seven categories.

Category	Enables You To
Accessibility	Set any keyboard shortcuts that can be used for the selected ASPX control.
Appearance	Set the appearance properties, such as font-style and color for the selected ASPX control.
Behavior	Allows you to set properties that determine the state of the ASPX control. It also allows you to set a tooltip for the control.
Data	Bind properties to expressions of the selected ASPX control.
Layout	Set the height and width of the selected ASPX control.
Misc	Set the property of an attribute that is not standards compliant.
Styles	Set styles that get applied when the mouse hovers over an ASPX control.

The src Attribute

The **src** attribute allows you to change the source of an image. Using the **src** attribute, you can swap images by specifying a new path for the image. This ensures that the other properties, such as the width and the height, of the image remain the same.

How to Work with Images

Procedure Reference: Replace an Image Using the Tag Properties Task Pane

To replace an image using the **Tag Properties** task pane:

1. On the web page, select the desired image.
2. Choose **Task Panes→Tag Properties.**
3. In the **Tag Properties** task pane, select the **src** attribute.
4. In the **src** attribute, click the browse button.
5. In the **Select File** dialog box, navigate to the desired image and click **Open** to replace the image.
6. Save and preview the page.

Alternate Method of Replacing an Image

An alternate method to replace an existing image is to delete the existing image and insert a new image. However, this method will not make the new image inherit the properties of the old one. The image will contain all the properties of the original image.

Procedure Reference: Edit an Image

To edit an image:

1. On the web page, select the image to be edited.
2. If necessary, choose **View→Toolbars→Pictures.**

3. On the **Pictures** toolbar, click the desired option to perform the corresponding editing task.

4. Save and preview the page.

Procedure Reference: Move Images in Multiple Editable Regions

To move images from one editable region to another:

1. On the web page, select the image to be moved.

2. Move the image to another editable region.

   - Drag the image to the desired editable region.

   - Or, cut the image and paste it in the editable region.

3. Save and preview the page.

ACTIVITY 3-6

Working with an Image

Data Files:

steve1.JPG

Before You Begin:

Open employeecorner.aspx.

Scenario:

You realize that a wrong image has been placed in the employeecorner.aspx page. You would like to replace that image with the correct one and also edit the picture so that it matches the requirements of the web page.

What You Do	How You Do It
1. Replace an image.	a. On the **employeecorner.aspx** page, select the image under the heading "Employee of the Month: Steve Miller".
	b. Choose **Task Panes→Tag Properties** to display the **Tag Properties** pane.
	c. In the **Tag Properties** task pane, select the **src** attribute and click the **Browse** button.

	d. In the **Select File** dialog box, navigate to the **C:\084721Data\Adding Content** folder.
	e. Select **steve1.JPG** and click **Open.**
	f. Close the **Tag Properties** task pane.
2. Crop the replaced image.	a. Choose **View→Toolbars→Pictures.**
	b. If necessary, reposition the toolbar to the desired location.
	c. On the **Pictures** toolbar, click the **Crop** button.

		d.	Place the mouse pointer at the top-left corner of the cropping frame and drag it upward toward the top-left corner of the picture so that the black border is excluded.
		e.	Place the mouse pointer at the bottom-right corner of the cropping frame and drag it downward toward the bottom-right of the picture so that the black border is excluded.
		f.	On the **Pictures** toolbar, click the **Crop** button.
		g.	Close the **Pictures** toolbar.
3.	Save and preview the page.	a.	Click the **Save** button.
		b.	In the **Save Embedded Files** dialog box, click **OK.**
		c.	Click the **Preview in Browser** button.
		d.	Close the browser window.
		e.	Close employeecorner.aspx.

Lesson 3 Follow-up

In this lesson, you added content to your website. Using SharePoint Designer, you can easily populate your web pages with text, tables, and images and enhance your website content.

1. **Which formatting option would you use frequently to format text on your web page?**

2. **When do you use tables on your site?**

Working with Cascading Style Sheets

Lesson Time: 1 hour(s)

Lesson Objectives:

In this lesson, you will use Cascading Style Sheets to format a SharePoint site.

You will:

- Get familiar with basic CSS concepts.
- Create an external style sheet.
- Create inline styles.
- Modify an external style sheet.

Introduction

You are now familiar with adding content to the website and formatting them. Another way of formatting web pages is through Cascading Style Sheets (CSS). CSS offer great flexibility and ease in customizing the web pages and in ensuring consistency in terms of site design and color scheme. In this lesson, you will customize your subsite using CSS.

Applying styles and formatting options to individual pages can be time consuming and there may not be consistency in the output. With CSS, you can save formatting options and apply them to multiple pages or to the entire website. CSS enables you to refine or format your web pages without the need for code-heavy documents and ensures that your website looks professional by applying consistent formatting throughout the website.

TOPIC A

Introduction to CSS

In the earlier lesson, you added and formatted text, tables, and images. But the changes you made to the web pages are localized. To make it effective at a global level, you need to use CSS. In this topic, you will familiarize yourself with the CSS concepts.

Many a times, certain design elements get repeated on a web page or a website. If you have to apply the same set of formatting options to the elements on every page, it is a repetitive and a tiring process. CSS can be used to design web pages without the need to repeat the same set of tasks. Even if you already know and work with CSS, getting acquainted with the basics of CSS will help you to use them more effectively.

Cascading Style Sheets

Cascading Style Sheet (*CSS*) is a style sheet language that can control the appearance of documents written in HTML, XML, or XHTML languages. It defines display features such as font types, color, and size, as well as text formatting features such as indentations and tabular presentation. The varied styles can be specified in one place and the content on the web pages can be formatted with the styles cascading throughout a page or a site.

 HTML, XML, and XHTML are otherwise called as markup languages.

Types of Cascading Style Sheets

There are three types of Cascading Style Sheets—external, internal or embedded, and inline.

Style Sheet Type	Description
External	The *External style sheet* is a style sheet in which styles are defined on a separate page. It has a .css file extension.
Internal or embedded	The *Internal style sheet* controls the formatting for the web page on which it is embedded.
Inline	The *Inline style sheet* affects only the HTML element (tag) that it is directly applied to.

 Sometimes, when more than one formatting option is applied to a block of text, SharePoint Designer applies the formatting using inline styles.

Styles

A *style* is a set of formatting options, which are defined in a CSS. A style can reside in an external, inline, or internal style sheet. There are three types of styles—class-based, element-based, and ID-based.

Style Type	*Description*
Class-based	This style can be applied for one or more elements on the page. Classes are represented with a . preceding the name. For example, .Imageborder is a style that you can create and apply to add a border to an image.
Element-based	This style is applied for every instance of a particular element. For example, a h2 style formats the content within all the h2 tags on the web page.
ID-based	This style is applied to name to distinguish an element from other similar elements. ID-based styles are identified with a # sign in front of the style name. For example, h2#red can be used to identify a single h2 tag among many h2 tags.

Cascading Style Sheet Rules

A *CSS rule* defines the syntax of a style. A CSS rule can be divided into two parts: *Selector* and *Declaration*. A selector selects the element to which you want to apply a style. The declaration has two parts: property and value. Property specifies the particular property or attribute of the element. A CSS rule can contain any number of properties and each property should be assigned a value.

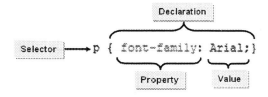

Figure 4-1: The parts of a CSS rule.

ACTIVITY 4-1

Getting Familiar with CSS

Scenario:

You're just getting started with CSS-based web development; you decide to test your understanding on basic CSS concepts.

---

1. **Which one of these is not a style sheet?**

   a) Class

   b) Inline

   c) External

   d) Internal

---

2. **True or False? An element-based style applies the style for every instance of a particular element.**

   ___ True

   ___ False

---

3. **Which of these options are style types?**

   a) Class

   b) External

   c) Element

   d) ID

---

4. **What defines the syntax of a style?**

   a) CSS

   b) Styles

   c) Selectors

   d) Rules

---

5. **What are the constituents of a declaration?**

   a) Selectors

   b) Value

   c) Rules

   d) Property

Handwritten notes at top:
Book " CSS the Missing Manual "
O'Reilly Press

"Professional mOSS Designer 200"
wrox

TOPIC B
Create an External Style Sheet

You familiarized yourself with the CSS concepts and now you are ready to work with CSS. You will begin by creating a simple style sheet. In this topic, you will create an external style sheet.

When working on a website, you come across a situation wherein some of the formatting style needs to be changed across all the web pages. This would mean manually duplicating the formatting style across all the pages on the website. It would be better if you had to update just one page and the change gets reflected across all the web pages. With external style sheets, you can modify and control all the color and typographical styles for as many pages as necessary from a single style sheet.

The Style Toolbar

The **Style** toolbar contains options that allow you to work with CSS styles.

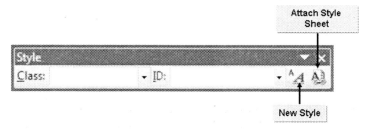

Handwritten note at right: Windows D (desktop)

Figure 4-2: The options in the Style toolbar.

The following table describes the options on the **Style** toolbar.

Option	Description
Class	Displays the list of classes.
ID	Allows you to display or create an ID.
New Style	Launches the **New Style** dialog box.
Attach Style Sheet	Launches the **Attach Style Sheet** dialog box.

The New Style Dialog Box

The **New Style** dialog box contains options that enable you to create a new CSS Style.

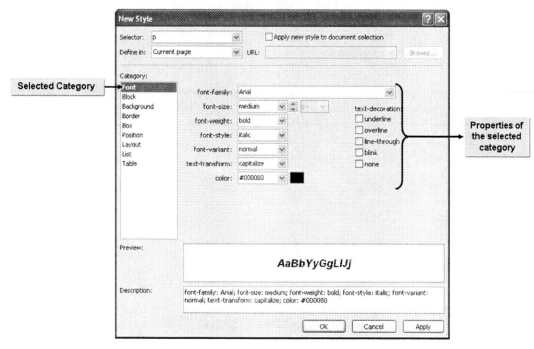

Figure 4-3: The options in the New Style dialog box.

The following table describes the options in the **New Style** dialog box.

Option	Description
Selector	Enables you to select an HTML element or to create an inline style. You can also name a class or ID by typing them out.
Define in	Enables you to specify the location of the style. It can be on the current page, in a new style sheet, or in an existing style sheet.
Category	Enables you to display and set the properties of a category.
Preview	Enables you to preview the style.
Description	Enables you to view the declaration part of the CSS rule.

Style Categories

The **New Style** dialog box lists a set of style categories using which you can define new styles.

Category	Description
Font	Displays all the properties related to font.
Block	Displays all the properties of block elements such as para and headings.
Background	Displays all the properties related to the background.
Border	Displays all the properties related to the border such as border style and border width for elements such as tables and images.
Box	Displays all the properties related to the box property for elements such as para or table.
Position	Displays all the properties related to the position of the elements.
Layout	Displays all the properties related to layouts.
List	Displays all the properties related to lists.
Table	Displays all the properties related to tables.

The Attach Style Sheet Dialog Box

The **Attach Style Sheet** dialog box is used to attach an external style sheet to all the pages, to the selected pages, or to the current page. You can specify the location of the style sheet in the **URL** text box or search for a style sheet using the **Browse** button. The **Attach Style Sheet** dialog box allows you to either link or import the style sheet.

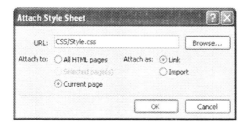

Figure 4-4: The options in the Attach Style Sheet dialog box.

Link vs. Import

A **Link** is an HTML tag that is used not only to link style sheets but also to link other pages. **Import** is a CSS rule that is used to import only style sheets. Generally, the inline style overwrites external and internal styles and the internal style overwrites the external style. The **Import** option supports this rule. When the **Link** option is used, the external style overwrites the internal style.

The Apply Styles Task Pane

The *Apply Styles task pane* provides you with options to create a new style, attach an external style sheet, and list all the styles available in different categories. The **Options** drop-down list allows you to change the category by which all the available styles are displayed and also specify which styles should be displayed in the task pane. A special option in the list is the **Preview Background Color,** which gives you a preview of how a background color will look against all the styles applied on the page.

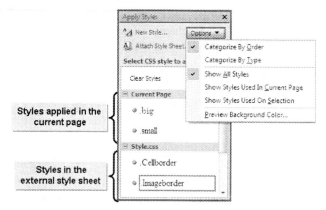

Figure 4-5: *The options in the Apply Styles task pane.*

How to Create an External Style Sheet

Procedure Reference: Build an External Style Sheet

To build an external style sheet:

1. Create a blank CSS page.

    • Choose **File→New→CSS.**

    • Or, on the **Common** or **Standard** toolbar, click the **New Document** drop-down arrow and choose **CSS.**

2. On the **Style** toolbar, click the **New Style** button.

3. Set the properties in the **New Style** dialog box.

    • In the **Selector** drop-down list, type the desired name or select an element.

    • Choose the desired category and set the desired properties.

4. Click **OK** to create a style.

5. If necessary, save the CSS file.

    • Save the CSS file to the website folder.

    • Or, create a new folder and save the CSS to the new folder.

6. If necessary, repeat steps 2, 3, and 4 to create another style.

Procedure Reference: Attach an External Style Sheet to a Web Page

To attach an external style sheet to a web page:

1. Open the desired web page or master page.

An external style sheet can be attached to a master page, so that all the pages attached to the master page are formatted. You can update files attached to a master page by clicking **Yes** in the **Microsoft Office SharePoint Designer** message box that appears while saving the master page. The content added to the content region also takes the formatting defined in the style sheet.

2. Display the **Attach Style Sheet** dialog box.
   - On the **Style** toolbar, click the **Attach Style Sheet** button.
   - Or, in the **Apply Styles/Manage Styles** task pane, click **Attach Style Sheet.**

3. Specify the location of the style sheet.
   - In the **URL** text box, type the path to the style sheet.
   - Or, click the **Browse** button and in the **Select Style Sheet** dialog box, navigate to the desired style sheet.

4. If necessary, select the **Import** option.

5. If necessary, select **All HTML pages** to attach the style sheet to all the web pages on the site.

 Multiple pages can be attached to the external style sheet by selecting multiple pages in the **Folder List** task pane and ensuring that the **Selected page(s)** option is selected in the **Attach Style Sheet** dialog box.

6. Click **OK** to attach the external style sheet.

Procedure Reference: Detach an External Style Sheet From a Web Page

To detach an external style sheet from a web page:

1. Open the desired web page or master page.

2. In the **Apply Styles** task pane, in the **Select CSS style to apply** list box, right-click the section header displaying the style sheet name and choose the desired option.
   - Choose **Remove Link** and in the **Microsoft Office SharePoint Designer** dialog box, click **Yes** to detach the style sheet from the current page.
   - Or, choose **Manage Style Sheet Links** and in the **Link Style Sheet** dialog box, select **All Pages, Selected Pages,** or **Current Page.** In the **URL** list box, select the style sheet that you want to detach, and click **Remove.**

3. Click **OK** to detach the style sheet from all the pages, selected pages, or current page that is linked to the CSS.

The Link Style Sheet Dialog Box

The **Link Style Sheet** dialog box allows you to manage style sheets linked to a web page. It contains options to detach the current page, the selected page or all pages linked to the CSS. The **URL** list box lists the links of the CSS linked to the page. The **Add, Move Down, Move Up, Remove,** and **Edit** buttons allow you to add, remove, edit, and even change the order of the style sheets.

ACTIVITY 4-2

Creating an External Style Sheet

Scenario:

You observe that certain elements such as headings and paragraph text get repeated on all the pages. You realize that formatting all the headings simultaneously will save you a lot of time. You would like to create an external style sheet and create styles for the headings and the text on the web pages.

What You Do	How You Do It
1. Display the **New Style** dialog box.	a. Choose **File→New→CSS**.
	b. Choose **View→Toolbars→Style**.
	c. If necessary, reposition the **Style** toolbar to the desired location.
	d. On the **Style** toolbar, click the **New Style** button.
2. Create a style for the paragraph element.	a. In the **New Style** dialog box, in the **Selector** drop-down list, scroll down and select **p**.
	b. In the **Font** category, in the **font-family** drop-down list, scroll down and select **Trebuchet MS**.
	c. From the **font-size** drop-down list, select **small**.
	d. In the **Category** list box, select **Box**.
	e. In the **padding** section, uncheck the **Same for all** check box.
	f. In the **right** text box, click and type *5*
	g. In the **left** text box, click and type *5* and click **OK**.

3. Create a style for the heading 2 element.

    a. On the **Style** toolbar, click the **New Style** button.

    b. In the **New Style** dialog box, in the **Selector** drop-down list, scroll down and select **h2.**

    c. In the **Font** category, in the **font-family** drop-down list, scroll down and select **Trebuchet MS.**

    d. In the **font-size** text box, click and type *26*

    e. From the **font-weight** drop-down list, select **bold.**

    f. In the **color** text box, click and type *#ED8512*

    g. In the **Category** list box, select **Box.**

    h. In the **padding** section, uncheck the **Same for all** check box.

    i. In the **left** text box, click and type *5* and click **OK.**

4. Save the style sheet.

    a. In the **Folder List** task pane title bar, click the **New Folder** button, type *CSS* and press **Enter.**

    b. Click the **Save** button.

    c. In the **Save As** dialog box, double-click the **CSS** folder.

    d. In the **File name** text box, triple-click and type *style*

    e. Click **Save.**

    f. Close style.css.

ACTIVITY 4-3

Attaching an External Style Sheet to the Master Page

Before You Begin:
Overwrite the css file in the subsite by importing style.css from the C:\084721Data\Working with Cascading Style Sheets folder, into the CSS folder of the HumanResources subsite.

Scenario:
You have created the external style sheet named style.css. Now, you want to attach the same to the pages on your subsite. You decide to link the external style sheet to the layout.master, so that all the web pages linked to the master page are formatted.

What You Do	How You Do It
1. Attach the style.css style sheet to the layout.master page.	a. In the **Folder List** task pane, double-click **employeecorner.aspx.**
	b. Observe the current formatting of the heading and the text.

Employee Corner

Welcome to the Employee Corner section. Here we place our spotlight on those people

	c. Close employeecorner.aspx.
	d. In the **Folder List** task pane, double-click **layout.master.**
	e. On the **Style** toolbar, click the **Attach Style Sheet** button.
	f. In the **Attach Style Sheet** dialog box, click **Browse.**
	g. In the **Select Style Sheet** dialog box, double-click the **CSS** folder.
	h. Select **style.css** and click **Open.**
	i. Click **OK.**
	j. Close the **Style** toolbar.

2.	Update the pages on the site.	a.	Click the **Save** button.
		b.	If necessary, in the **Microsoft Office SharePoint Designer** message box, click **Yes** to update the files attached to the layout.master page.
		c.	If necessary, in the **Microsoft Office SharePoint Designer** message box, click **Close.**
		d.	Close layout.master.
3.	View the changes applied to the pages.	a.	In the **Folder List** task pane, double-click **employeecorner.aspx.**
		b.	Observe that the formatting of the heading and the paragraph text has changed and reflects the styles that you had specified in style.css.

Employee Corner

Welcome to the Employee Corner section. Here we place our spotlight on those people

		c.	In the **Folder List** task pane, double-click **hremployees.aspx.**

HR Employees

We take pride in our people who are effectively the driving force behind the seamless

		d.	Observe that similar formatting has been applied for this web page also.
		e.	Close hremployees.aspx.

TOPIC C
Create Internal Styles

You created an external style sheet and attached it to the web pages. But, there may be times when a page might warrant a different look from other pages. In this topic, you will create an internal style sheet.

You may need to format a single web page for a number of reasons. The page may need some unique formatting or you may prefer to test a formatting or a layout option on a page before you implement it on all the other pages. By creating an internal style sheet, you can apply formatting for a web page and make it standout from the rest of the pages.

How to Create Internal Styles

Procedure Reference: Create an Internal Style Sheet

To create an internal style sheet:

1. Open the desired web page.
2. Display the **New Style** dialog box.
   - On the **Style** toolbar, click the **New Style** button.
   - Or, in the **Apply Styles** task pane, click the **New Style** link.
3. Set the properties in the **New Style** dialog box.
   a. In the **Selector** drop-down list, type the desired name or select an element.
   b. Choose the desired category and set the desired properties.
4. Click **OK** to create a style.
5. If necessary, repeat steps 2, 3, and 4 to create other styles in the internal style sheet.

ACTIVITY 4-4

Creating an Internal Style Sheet

Before You Begin:

Ensure that the **employeecorner.aspx** page is open.

Scenario:

You want to add borders for images and format some text on web pages that has already been formatted using the external style sheet. But, you are not sure about the outcome. So, you decide to experiment with the new styles on just the **employeecorner.aspx** page to test the output of the new styles.

What You Do	How You Do It
1. Create a class-based style for the border of an image.	a. Choose **Task Panes→Apply Styles.**
	b. In the **Apply Styles** task pane, click the **New Style** link.
	c. In the **New Style** dialog box, in the **Selector** text box, after the period, type *imageborder*
	d. In the **Category** list box, select **Border.**
	e. In the **border-style** section, from the **top** drop-down list, select **solid.**
	f. In the **border-width** section, in the **top** text box, click and type *2*
	g. In the **border-color** section, in the **top** text box, click and type *#6699FF*
	h. Click **OK** to create the `.imageborder` style.
	i. Observe that the `.imageborder` style is listed in the **Current Page** section of the **Apply Styles** task pane.

2. Apply the `.imageborder` style.

   a. Select the first image on the employee corner page.

   b. In the **Apply Styles** task pane, click `.imageborder.`

   c. Similarly, apply the `.imageborder` style to the second image on the page.

   d. Save employeecorner.aspx.

   e. Click the **Preview in Browser** button.

   f. Close the browser window.

3. Create a class-based style for high-lighting text.

   a. In the **Apply Styles** task pane, click the **New Style** link.

   b. In the **New Style** dialog box, in the **Selector** text box, after the period, type *fontstyle*

   c. In the **Font** category, in the **font-family** drop-down list, scroll down and select **Trebuchet MS.**

   d. In the **font-size** text box, click and type *14*

   e. From the **font-weight** drop-down list, select **bold.**

   f. In the **color** text box, click and type *#6699FF*

   g. Click **OK** to create the `.fontstyle` style.

4. Apply the `.fontstyle` style.

   a. Shift-click the text "Employee: Steve Miller" to select it.

   b. In the **Apply Styles** task pane, click `.fontstyle.`

   c. Similarly, apply the `.fontstyle` style to the text: "Team award: The Finance Team".

   d. Save employeecorner.aspx.

   e. Click the **Preview in Browser** button.

   f. Close the browser window.

TOPIC D
Modify External Style Sheets

You are now familiar with the creation of internal and external style sheets. Based on some specific requirements, you may have to make some changes to the styles in the style sheets. In this topic, you will modify an external style sheet.

While creating a website, you may have to make a number of modifications such as changing the page order, or rearranging content on the web pages. The same holds true for style sheets also. Sometimes, styles used earlier might not be needed at a later stage. By modifying the style sheet, you can meet the new requirements of the website.

SharePoint Themes

A SharePoint theme is a design template that provides a consistent look and feel to the pages in a website. The theme determines the colors and fonts that are used throughout the pages of the site. Using SharePoint Designer, you can access the style sheet that controls the themes, thereby modifying them easily.

The Manage Styles Task Pane

The *Manage Styles task pane* contains options that enable you to manage styles that are applied to a web page. The **Manage Styles** task pane is primarily used to move and arrange styles used on a web page. It provides most of the options available in the **Apply Styles** task pane. In addition, it enables you to ungroup selectors if they are grouped and to turn off the preview feature.

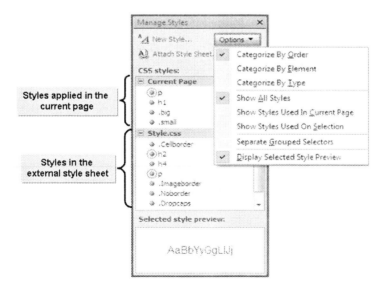

Figure 4-6: The options in the Manage Styles task pane.

How to Modify External Style Sheets

Procedure Reference: Modify an External Style Sheet

To modify an external style sheet:

1. Open an external style sheet.

2. Move an internal style from a web page to the external style sheet.

   a. Open a web page linked to an external style sheet.

   b. In the **Manage Styles** task pane, drag a style from the **Current Page** category to the **css** category.

 An external style can also be moved to the internal style sheet by using the **Manage Styles** task pane.

3. Modify a style.

   a. In the **Manage Styles** task pane, right-click the desired style and choose **Modify Style.**

   b. In the **Modify Style** dialog box, modify the style.

 The **Modify Style** dialog box has the same options as the **Apply Styles** dialog box.

4. If necessary, delete a style.

   - In the **Manage Styles** dialog box, select a style and press **Delete.**

   - Or, in the **Manage Styles** task pane, right-click a style and choose **Delete.**

Procedure Reference: Modify the Theme Using CSS

To modify the theme using CSS:

1. Open a top-level site.

2. If necessary, display the **Apply Styles** task pane.

3. Edit the theme using CSS.

   - Edit the style sheet using the **Manage Styles**s task pane.

     a. Display the **Manage Styles** task pane.

     b. If necessary, in the **Selected style preview** section, preview the selected style.

     c. In the **Manage Styles** task pane, in the **CSS styles** section, right-click on the desired style and choose **Modify Style.**

     d. In the **Modify Style** dialog box, select the necessary options to make the required changes and then click **OK.**

     e. If necessary, in the **Manage Styles** task pane, click the **New style** link and create a new style and apply it to the desired element on the page.

   - Or, edit the style sheet in the **Code** view.

     a. Open the **core.css** style sheet.

- In the **Apply Styles** task pane, double-click the **core.css** section header to open the **core.css** style sheet.
- Or, in the **Folder List** task pane, navigate to the **[site name]/_styles** folder and open **core.css.**

b. In the **core.css** style sheet, navigate to the appropriate line and type the necessary code to change the color or font scheme of the region.

4. If necessary, save the CSS and the master pages.

5. If necessary, preview the pages that are attached to the modified master page.

Default Regions on a Master Page

The default master page is divided into different regions or cells. The formatting of these regions are controlled by styles specified in the default style sheet (**core.css**). These styles in the style sheet collectively contribute to the creation of the theme of the web page. You can modify the theme by editing the default styles.

The following table lists some of the regions on the default master page.

Region	Allows You To
.ms-HoverCellActive, .ms-SpLinkButtonInActive	Set the border, margin, font color, alignment, and background of the global links.
	Welcome GLOBAL\user1 ▾
.ms-sbcell	Set the padding, border, and white space for the wrapper around search input button and advanced search link.
	This Site ▼
.ms-siteaction, .ms-siteaction a	Set the font size, family, weight, and color text decoration for the site action text.
	Site Actions ▾
.ms-quicklaunchheader	Set the padding, font weight, color, size, text decoration, and background for the header of the **Quick Launch** bar.
	View All Site Content
.ms-navheader	Set the background border, padding, font weight, color, and text decoration for the navigation headers.
	Documents

Region	Allows You To
.ms-navitem	Set the background, padding, font family, color, and text decoration for the sub navigation items that comes under navigation headers.
	■ Calendar ■ Tasks
.ms-recyclebin	Set the background, width, border, padding, font weight, color, and text decoration for the recycle bin.
	Recycle Bin
.ms-pagetitle	Set the font color, family, size, weight, and margin for the title text of the page.
	Tasks
.ms-pagebreadcrumb	Set the padding, border, the font size, color, text decoration, and background for the breadcrumb in the navigation area.
	Team Site > Team Discussion
.ms-menutoolbar	Set the border, height, and the background for the toolbar menu.
	New ▼ Actions ▼ Settings ▼
.ms-toolbar	Set the font family, size, color, text decoration, background, and border for the wrapping table cell of the toolbar.
	Title Assigned To
.ms-calheader	Set the background for the calendar header.
	← → February, 2008 Sunday Monday

ACTIVITY 4-5

Modifying an External Style Sheet

Before you Begin:

Ensure that the **employeecorner.aspx** page is open.

Scenario:

You are satisfied with the formatting that you applied to the **employee corner** page. You want to follow the same formatting pattern for the rest of the pages on the site. You would like to make the styles in the internal sheet accessible to the rest of the pages.

What You Do	How You Do It
1. Move the internal styles to the style.css style sheet.	a. Choose **Task Panes→Manage Styles.**
	b. In the **Manage Styles** task pane, double-click the **style.css** section header to open the **style.css** stylesheet.
	c. Observe the styles.
	d. On the top of the editing window, select the **employeecorner.aspx** page.
	e. In the **Manage Styles** task pane, in the **Current Page** section, select `.imageborder` and shift-click `.fontstyle`.
	f. Drag the selected styles to the **style.css** section below the existing styles.

	g. On the top of the editing window, select the **style.css** page.
	h. In the **style.css** stylesheet, scroll down.

i. Observe that both the internal styles have been moved to the external style sheet.

```
.imageborder {
    border: 2px solid #6699FF;
}
.fontstyle {
    font-family: "Trebuchet MS";
    font-size: 14px;
    font-weight: bold;
    font-style: italic;
    color: #6699FF;
}
```

2. Modify a style in the external style sheet.

a. In the **Manage Styles** task pane, right-click `.imageborder` and choose **Modify Style.**

b. In the **Modify Style** dialog box, select the **Border** category.

c. In the **border-color** section, in the **top** text box, click and type **#ED8512** and click **OK** to change the border color.

d. Save style.css and close it.

e. Observe that the border of the images on the employee corner page has been changed.

f. Save employeecorner.aspx.

g. Click the **Preview in Browser** button.

ACTIVITY 4-6
Modifying the Theme Using CSS

Scenario:
You have created the styles of your choice and have formatted the text and images by applying the styles. You want to edit the default master page theme of the top-level site to match the color scheme of the subsite.

What You Do	How You Do It
1. Open the **core.css** style sheet of the top-level site.	a. Choose **File→Open Site.**
	b. In the **Open Site** dialog box, in the **Web Sites** folder, select your top-level site and click **Open.**
	c. In the **Folder List** task pane, navigate to the **http://[site name]/_catalogs/ masterpage (Master Page Gallery)** folder and open the **default.master** page.
	d. If necessary, display the **Manage Styles** task pane.
	e. In the **Manage Styles** task pane, double-click the **core.css - <SharePoint:csslink/>** section header to open the **core.css** style sheet.
2. Modify the background and the text in the **Quick Launch** bar.	a. In the **core.css** style sheet, right-click and choose **Go To Line.**
	b. In the **Go To Line** dialog box, in the **Enter line number** text box, type *745* and click **OK.**
	c. Observe that a preview of the selected style is displayed in the **Selected style preview** section of the **Manage Styles** task pane.

d. In the **core.css** stylesheet, double-click the background-color value and after #, type *2879B8* to set the background color as blue.

```
.ms-quicklaunch table.ms-navheader td,.ms-navheader2 td,.ms-quicklaunch span.ms-navheader{
background-color:#2879B8;
border-top:solid 1px #C2F8FF;
border-left:solid 1px #C2F8FF;
padding:1px 4px 4px 4px;
}
```

e. Press the **Down Arrow** key.

f. Observe that a preview of the modified style is displayed in the **Selected style preview** section of the **Manage Styles** task pane.

g. Go to line *854.*

h. In the **Manage Styles** task pane, in the **CSS styles** section right-click the `.ms-navheader a, .ms-navheader2 a` style and choose **Modify Style.**

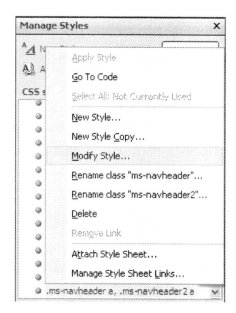

i. In the **Modify Style** dialog box, in the **Font** category, from the **font-family** drop-down list, select **Arial.**

j. Click in the **font-size** text box and type *12*

k. In the **font-weight** drop-down list, scroll up and select **normal.**

l. In the **color** text box, click and type *#FFFFFF* to set the font color as white and click **OK.**

m. Save core.css.

n. In the **Stylesheet Customization Warning** message box, click **Yes.**

3. Preview the changes on the **default.aspx** page.

   a. On the top of the editing window, select the **default.master** page.

   b. Observe that the changes have been applied to the **Quick Launch** bar.

   c. If necessary, save default.master.

   d. In the **Folder List** task pane, select **default.aspx** and click the **Preview in Browser** button.

   e. Observe that the changes have been updated in the default.aspx also.

   f. Close the browser window.

   g. Choose **File→Exit.**

Lesson 4 Follow-up

In this lesson, you formatted a website using Cascading Style Sheets. CSS offers great flexibility and ease in designing effective web pages and ensures that your website looks professional because of consistency in formatting.

1. **When building a website, what do you think are the benefits of using CSS when compared to that of HTML?**

2. **What kind of a style sheet would you use to ensure consistency across the web pages?**

5 | Adding Basic Functionality to Web Pages

Lesson Time: 1 hour(s), 5 minutes

Lesson Objectives:

In this lesson, you will add basic functionality to web pages.

You will:

- Work with hyperlinks.
- Create a hotpsot.
- Add bookmark links.
- Add an interactive button.
- Add a behavior.

Introduction

You have created and formatted web pages. To build a functional website, you need to link all the web pages logically. In this lesson, you will link pages using hyperlinks, behaviors, and interactive buttons.

As you keep adding web pages to your website, it is essential that you link the pages logically with each other. Otherwise, users will have to type the complete URL of every web page they want to visit; they could enter an incorrect URL and end up viewing an error page. SharePoint Designer provides you with several options to add links to web pages.

TOPIC A

Add Hyperlinks

You have created web pages that have images and text. To aid in the proper presentation of the content, you need to connect the web pages through hyperlinks. In this topic, you will link the pages of your site by adding hyperlinks.

The advantage of a website is that you can skip from page to page by just clicking a link. By adding hyperlinks to your web pages, you'll enable your users to easily navigate through your site and quickly locate pertinent information.

Hyperlinks

Definition:

A *hyperlink* is a text or an image link on a web page. It connects to another section of the same page or another web page. A typical hyperlink is composed of the text that contains the link and the destination address or URL of the target page. By default, hyperlinks on a page are shown as blue, underlined text and a hand cursor appears on mouse over.

Example:

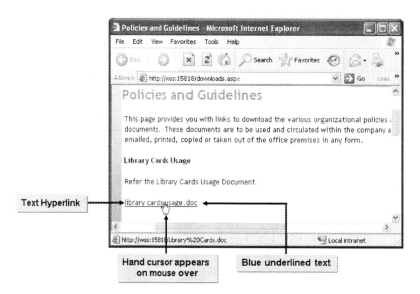

Linking URLs

Inside a link is a URL that provides the location of the targeted resource. The syntax for a URL is `protocol://servername/foldername/filename`. In the context of the web, the protocol is generally HyperText Transfer Protocol (HTTP). The rest of the URL tells the browser where to find the file. After the colon is the name of the server, host, or domain name, that provides the file. Following the server name is the path—usually a folder and a file name.

Relative and Absolute Addresses

URL addresses can either be relative or absolute. Relative addresses are used for linking resources that reside within a web's folder structure. For this URL, the protocol and the server name are omitted and only the path is used. Absolute references are always used for resources outside your web. These URLs must be complete, and should contain the protocol, server location, and file path details.

The Insert Hyperlink Dialog Box

The various options in the **Insert Hyperlink** dialog box help you add hyperlinks to your web pages.

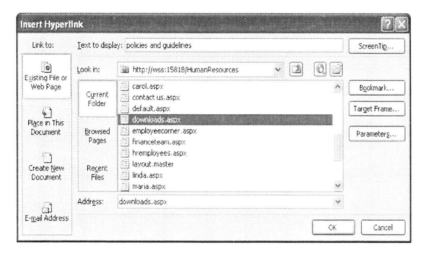

Figure 5-1: The options in the Insert Hyperlink dialog box.

The following table lists the options in the **Insert Hyperlink** dialog box.

Option	Enables You To
The **The Link to** section	Link the hyperlink to an existing file or web page, a place in the same document, a web page on a different site, a new document, or to an email address.
The **Text to display** text box	Enter the text for a hyperlink. This is the text that will be clicked on the web page.
The **ScreenTip** button	Enter a screen tip that will be displayed when you place the mouse pointer over the link.
The **Bookmark** button	Create a hyperlink to a selected bookmark.
The **Target Frame** button	Select a target frame on a frames page.
The **Parameters** button	Set the hyperlink parameters.

Hyperlink States

The status of a hyperlink is called the hyperlink state and it is defined by user activity. There are four different *hyperlink states.*

 If you were using Cascading Style Sheets (CSS) to format hyperlinks, you can go a step forward to define the font size, family, and other text properties for each of these states.

Hyperlink State	Description
Hyperlink	The default state of the hyperlink when it is not selected.
Hovered hyperlink	The dynamic state of the hyperlink when you hover the mouse pointer over the link and see a pointed finger symbol being displayed.
Active hyperlink	The dynamic state of the hyperlink when the mouse pointer is clicked on the link.
Visited hyperlink	The static state of the hyperlink after it has been clicked.

How to Add Hyperlinks

Procedure Reference: Create a Text/Image Hyperlink

To create a text/image hyperlink:

1. Select the desired text or image.
2. Open the **Insert Hyperlink** dialog box.
    - Choose **Insert→Hyperlink.**
    - On the **Standard** toolbar, click the **Insert Hyperlink** button.
    - Right-click the selected text and choose **Hyperlink.**
    - Or, press **Ctrl+K.**
3. Enter the link's destination.
    - If the link's destination is outside your website, enter the full URL.
    - If the link's destination is within your website, enter the destination file name.
    - Or, browse and select the destination file.
4. If desired, to link to a new document that is not yet created, type in the name of the new document. This option will create a new document and will add a link to it.
5. If desired, add a screen tip.
    a. Click the **ScreenTip** button.
    b. In the **Set Hyperlink ScreenTip** dialog box, in the **ScreenTip text** text box, type the desired text.
    c. Click **OK.**
6. In the **Insert Hyperlink** dialog box, click **OK.**

7.   If necessary, save and preview the page.

Procedure Reference: Create a Downloadable Hyperlink

To create a downloadable hyperlink:

1.   Import the files that need to be downloaded.

2.   Open the web page where you want to create hyperlinks for the downloadable files.

3.   From the **Folder List** task pane, drag the file that needs to go as downloadable onto the web page.

> Multiple files in the **Folder List** task pane can be selected and dragged onto the web page. SharePoint Designer creates links for each of the files separately.

4.   If necessary, display a different text for the downloadable link.

   a.   Open the **Edit Hyperlink** dialog box.

   •   Place the insertion point on the downloadable hyperlink and choose **Insert→ Hyperlink.**

   •   Place the insertion point on the downloadable hyperlink and on the **Standard** toolbar, click the **Insert Hyperlink** button.

   •   Right-click the link and choose **Hyperlink Properties.**

   •   Or, place the insertion point on the downloadable hyperlink and press **Ctrl+K.**

   b.   In the **Edit Hyperlink** dialog box, in the **Text to display** text box, type the desired text you want to be displayed as a link.

5.   If necessary, save and preview the page.

Screen Tips

A screen tip, by providing information about a link, can help Internet Explorer users navigate through your site. This information is displayed when users hover their mouse pointer over the link.

> Screen tips are not supported by all browsers.

> You can test a screen tip in the **Preview** mode.

Downloadable Files

Several file types can be set as downloadable files. Some of the file types include .doc, .docx, .pdf, .txt, .zip, .rar, .iso, and .wmv.

Procedure Reference: Create an Email Hyperlink

To create an email hyperlink:

1. Type the desired email address and press **Enter.**

 When text that resembles an email address is typed, SharePoint Designer identifies and converts the text to an email hyperlink as soon as the **Enter** key is pressed. Any text that contains the @ symbol is treated as an email hyperlink.

2. Click the email hyperlink.
3. Open the **Edit Hyperlink** dialog box.
4. In the **Subject** text box, type the desired subject line.
5. Click **OK** for the changes to take effect.
6. If necessary, save and preview the page.

Procedure Reference: Edit a Hyperlink

To edit a hyperlink:

1. Select the text or image that contains the link.
2. Open the **Edit Hyperlink** dialog box.
3. Edit the hyperlink.
   - In the **Address** text box, type a new address to change the link's destination.
   - Click the **Remove Hyperlink** button to remove the hyperlink.
4. Click **OK** for the changes to take effect.
5. If necessary, save and preview the page.

Procedure Reference: Format Text Hyperlinks Using the Page Properties Dialog Box

To format text hyperlinks using the **Page Properties** dialog box:

1. Open the web page on which the text hyperlinks to be formatted are located.
2. Open the Page Properties dialog box.
3. In the **Page Properties** dialog box, click the Formatting tab.
4. In the **Colors** section, select the appropriate colors for the various states: Hyperlink, Visited hyperlink, Active hyperlink, and Hovered hyperlink boxes. Click OK.
5. If necessary, save and preview the page.

 When a web page is linked to a master page, the formatting options in the **Page Properties** dialog box are disabled. The desired formatting options will have to be set in the master page for the changes to get reflected on the web pages linked to the master page. This ensures consistent formatting throughout the site.

Procedure Reference: Format Text Hyperlinks Using CSS

To format text hyperlinks using CSS:

1. Open the web page on which the text hyperlinks to be formatted are located.

2. Select the location of the styles.

    ● To add hyperlink styles to an internal CSS on a web page, open the desired web page.

    ● To add hyperlink styles to an external CSS, open the desired .css file.

3. Open the New Style dialog box.

4. In the **New Style** dialog box, from the **Selector** drop-down list, select the desired options.

    ● Select **a** to set the default appearance of a hyperlink.

    ● Select **a: link** to set the appearance of hyperlinks that haven't been clicked.

    ● Select **a: visited** to set the appearance of hyperlinks that have been clicked.

    ● Select **a: hover** to set the appearance of a hyperlink when the pointer is over the hyperlink.

    ● Select **a: active** to set the appearance of a hyperlink when clicked.

 The above-mentioned order of the hyperlink states should be maintained so that the hyperlinks states work. If the order is changed, then some of the hyperlink states might not work.

5. Set the desired properties and values for the selector.

6. Click **OK.**

ACTIVITY 5-1

Creating a Hyperlink

Data Files:

maria.aspx, susan.aspx, linda.aspx, carol.aspx, maria2.jpg, susan2.jpg, linda2.jpg, carol2.jpg

1. Import the pages **maria.aspx, susan.aspx, linda.aspx,** and **carol.aspx** and the images, **maria2.jpg, susan2.jpg, linda2.jpg,** and **carol2.jpg** from the **C:\084721Data\Adding Basic Functionality** folder into the HumanResources subsite.

2. Move the images into the **images** folder.

3. Close the **Manage Styles** task pane group.

Scenario:

You have completed developing the pages for your subsite. You decide to create hyperlinks to link the relevant pages. You want to create hyperlinks for the following pages.

● As the text in the terms and conditions page references the downloads page, you will link it to the **downloads.aspx** page.

● For the employees to easily contact the HR through email and get their doubts clarified, you will provide an email hyperlink on the **contactus.aspx** page.

● As the details of the award winners in the employees corner page are given in separate pages, you will link the photographs to their respective details pages.

What You Do	How You Do It
1. Create a text hyperlink.	a. In the **Folder List** task pane, double-click **termsandconditions.aspx.**
	b. On the **termsandconditions.aspx** page, select the text "policies and guidelines".
	c. Choose **Insert→Hyperlink.**
	d. Verify that in the **Insert Hyperlink** dialog box, in the **Link to** section, the **Existing File or Web Page** button is selected.
	e. In the **Insert Hyperlink** dialog box, in the **Current Folder** list box, scroll down, select **downloads.aspx,** and click **OK.**
	f. Save termsandconditions.aspx.

2.	Test the text hyperlink.	a.	Click the **Preview in Browser** button.
		b.	On the terms and conditions page, click the "policies and guidelines" hyperlink to open the downloads page.
		c.	Close the browser window.
		d.	Close termsandconditions.aspx.
3.	Create an email hyperlink.	a.	In the **Folder List** task pane, double-click **contactus.aspx.**
		b.	Click after the text "your comments to:".
		c.	Press the **Spacebar,** type *queries@ourglobalcompany.com* and press **Enter.**
		d.	Right-click "queries@ourglobalcompany.com" and choose **Hyperlink Properties.**
		e.	In the **Edit Hyperlink** dialog box, in the **Link to** section, verify that the **E-mail Address** button is selected.
		f.	In the **Subject** text box, click and type *Regarding:* and click **OK.**
		g.	Save contactus.aspx.
4.	Test the email hyperlink.	a.	Click the **Preview in Browser** button.
		b.	Click "queries@ourglobalcompany.com".
		c.	If necessary, in the **Internet Explorer Security** message box, click **Allow.**
		d.	Observe that your email client opens up with the **To** field populated with the text "queries@ourglobalcompany.com" and the **Subject** field populated with the text "Regarding:".
		e.	Close your email client and, in the **Microsoft Office Outlook** message box, click **No.**
		f.	Close the browser window.
		g.	Close contactus.aspx.

5.	Create an image hyperlink.	a.	In the **Folder List** task pane, double-click **employeecorner.aspx.**
		b.	On the **employeecorner.aspx** page, select the first image and choose **Insert→ Hyperlink.**
		c.	In the **Insert Hyperlink** dialog box, in the **Link to** section, select the **Existing File or Web Page** button.
		d.	In the **Current Folder** list box, scroll down, select **steve.aspx** and click **OK.**
		e.	Similarly, link the second image to the **financeteam.aspx** page.
		f.	Save employeecorner.aspx.
6.	Test the image hyperlink.	a.	Click the **Preview in Browser** button.
		b.	Click the image of Steve Miller to open the **steve.aspx** page.
		c.	Close the browser window.
		d.	Close employeecorner.aspx.

ACTIVITY 5-2

Creating a Downloadable Hyperlink

Before You Begin:

From the C:\084721Data\Adding Basic Functionality folder, import the library cards usage.doc, desktop usage.doc, leave policy.doc, travel policy.doc, and the equal employment opportunity.doc files into the HumanResources subsite.

Scenario:

You want to provide the documents on organizational policies and guidelines as links to the users so that they can download the files to their computers and read it whenever necessary.

What You Do	How You Do It
1. Add downloadable hyperlinks.	a. In the **Folder List** task pane, double-click the **downloads.aspx** page.
	b. From the **Folder List** task pane, drag **library cards usage.doc** and place it after the text, "Refer the Library Cards Usage Document."
	Library Cards Usage
	Refer the Library Cards Usage Document.
	library cards usage.doc
	c. Similarly, from the **Folder List** task pane, add the desktop usage.doc, leave policy.doc, travel policy.doc, and the equal employment opportunity.doc files after their respective sections on the **downloads.aspx** page.
	d. Save downloads.aspx.

2. Test the downloadable hyperlink.

   a. Click the **Preview in Browser** button.

   b. Click "library cards usage.doc".

   c. In the **File Download** dialog box, click **Open** to open **library cards usage.doc.**

   d. On the **Quick Access Toolbar,** click the **Save** button.

   e. In the **Save As** dialog box, in the left pane, click **Desktop** and then click **Save.**

   f. If necessary, in the **Download Complete** dialog box, click **Open.**

   g. Close the Word document and the browser window.

   h. Close downloads.aspx.

ACTIVITY 5-3

Formatting Text Hyperlinks

Before You Begin:

Since we have tested the hyperlinks in the first activity, the hyperlinks will be in the visited state. In order to make the hyperlinks active, you have to clear the cache.

1. Open Internet Explorer, and from the **Tools** drop-down list, choose **Internet Options.**

2. In the **Internet Options** dialog box, on the **General** tab, click **Delete Cookies, Delete files,** and **Clear History.**

In case of IE 7.0, in the **Browsing History** section, click **Delete** and then click **Delete files, Delete cookies,** and **Delete history.**

3. Close the dialog boxes and the browser window.

Scenario:

You find that the default format of the text hyperlinks does not suit your website. So, you decide to set various hyperlink states and make hyperlinks more suitable to your website.

What You Do	How You Do It
1. Display the **Page Properties** dialog box.	a. In the **Folder List** task pane, double-click **layout.master.**
	b. Choose **File→Properties.**
2. Set the hyperlink color properties.	a. In the **Page Properties** dialog box, select the **Formatting** tab.
	b. From the **Hyperlink** drop-down list, in the **Standard Colors** section, select **Navy.**
	c. From the **Visited hyperlink** drop-down list, in the **Standard Colors** section, select **Maroon.**
	d. From the **Hovered hyperlink** drop-down list, in the **Standard Colors** section, select **Blue.**
	e. Click **OK.**
	f. Save layout.master.

3. Test the new settings.

a. In the **Folder List** task pane, select **termsandconditions.aspx.**

b. Click the **Preview in Browser** button.

c. Place the mouse over the "policies and guidelines" hyperlink and observe that the color changes to blue.

d. Click the "policies and guidelines" hyperlink.

e. In the Internet Explorer browser window, click the **Back** button.

f. Observe that the hyperlink, "policies and guidelines" is maroon in color to indicate the visited state.

g. Close the browser window.

TOPIC B
Create a Hotspot

Your web pages now contain hyperlinks. Another commonly used type of image link is a hotspot. In this topic, you'll create hotspot links to images on your web pages.

Assume that you own a tourism website that provides a write-up for each of the various states in the country. Currently, you have a web page in which a list of the names of the states has been provided. Users can click each of these links to view its description. Will it not be a better idea, if you can provide users with a map and ask them to click on a particular state to view its description? Hotspots help you achieve this.

Hotspots

A *hotspot* is a hyperlink that is defined for a specific part of an image. You can use the **Pictures** toolbar to create a hotspot. The hotspot can be rectangular, circular, or polygonal. The **Insert Hyperlink** dialog box appears as soon as you draw the hotspot and it enables you to set a target for the link. An image can contain more than one hotspot.

How to Create a Hotspot

Procedure Reference: Create a Hotspot

To add a hotspot to an image:

1. On your web page, select the picture to which you want to add a hotspot.
2. On the **Pictures** toolbar, select the **Rectangular Hotspot,** or the **Circular Hotspot,** or the **Polygonal Hotspot** button.
3. On the selected image, click and drag the mouse pointer to the required location to define the hotspot region.
4. In the **Insert Hyperlink** dialog box, locate the file you want to link to and then click **OK.**
5. If necessary, save and test the hotspot.

ACTIVITY 5-4

Adding a Hotspot to an Image

Scenario:

In order to serve the users better, you have decided to add a link to the customer service web page on your home page. Instead of providing a regular text link, you decide to make it more attractive by providing the link on an image on the home page.

What You Do	How You Do It
1. Add a hotspot link.	a. On the **layout.master** page, scroll to the right and select the contact us image.
	b. Choose **View→Toolbars→Pictures.**
	c. If necessary, reposition the **Pictures** toolbar to the desired location.
	d. On the **Pictures** toolbar, select the **Rectangular Hotspot** button. 
	e. Observe that the mouse pointer changes to a pencil cursor when hovered over the selected image.
	f. Using the pencil cursor, draw a rectangle encompassing the text "Contact Us".

Contact Us

	g. If necessary, in the **Insert Hyperlink** dialog box, verify that the **Existing File or Web Page** button is selected.
	h. In the **Insert Hyperlink** dialog box, from the **Current Folder** list box, select **contactus.aspx,** and click **OK.**
	i. Close the **Pictures** toolbar.

 If the toolbar has been docked, choose **View→Toolbar→Pictures** to close it.

		j.	Save layout.master.
2.	Test the hotspot link.	a.	In the **Folder List** task pane, select **hremployees.aspx** and click the **Preview in Browser** button.
		b.	In the browser window, scroll down and then on the contact us image, click the words "Contact Us" to open the **contactus.aspx** page.
		c.	Close the browser window.
		d.	Close layout.master.

TOPIC C
Add Bookmark Links

You've added links that connect several of the pages in your website. However, there might be instances where you may want to connect two different sections of the same web page. In this topic, you'll add bookmark links to a web page.

In a corporate intranet or personal website, there may be times when you may want to place a large amount of content on a single web page. But without links to specific locations within the web page, your users might not be able to easily locate the information that they are looking for. Adding bookmark links to the web page will help your users navigate through a lengthy web page and locate the information they are looking for.

Bookmark Links

A *bookmark link* connects to a specific target location within the same page. Bookmark links have two parts. The first part is a *bookmark,* which is a label given to a specific section of a web page. The other is a hyperlink, which connects to a bookmark targeting a specific region on a page.

The Bookmark Dialog Box

The **Bookmark** dialog box helps you add and remove bookmarks and navigate to an existing bookmark on a given web page. After selecting an existing bookmark, you can navigate to the specific section by clicking the **Go To** button. By clicking the **Clear** button, you can delete the currently selected bookmark.

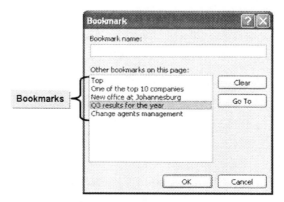

Figure 5-2: The options in the Bookmark dialog box.

How to Add Bookmark Links

Procedure Reference: Add a Bookmark Link

To add bookmark links in your web page:

1. Add a bookmark or bookmarks to an existing web page.

    a. Navigate to the location that needs to be bookmarked.

    b. Choose **Insert→Bookmark** or press **Ctrl+G.**

    c. In the **Bookmark** dialog box, in the **Bookmark name** text box, specify a bookmark name.

    d. Click **OK.**

2. Select the desired text that needs to be linked to the bookmark.

3. Open the **Insert Hyperlink** dialog box.

4. In the **Existing File or Web Page** section, click **Bookmark.**

5. In the **Select Place in Document** dialog box, select a bookmark and click **OK.**

6. If necessary, save and preview the page.

ACTIVITY 5-5
Adding Bookmark Links

Scenario:
The news release web page runs into numerous sections making the page lengthy. To help
users navigate between the table of contents and the various sections on this web page, you
have decided to add appropriate bookmark links.

What You Do	How You Do It
1. Add bookmarks to the **newsrelease.aspx** page.	a. In the **Folder List** task pane, double-click **newsrelease.aspx**.
	b. In the second line, triple-click the text "Our Global Company selected as one of the top 10 consulting companies" to select it.
	c. **Choose Insert→Bookmark.**
	d. In the **Bookmark** dialog box, in the **Bookmark name** text box, **type *Top* and click OK.**
	e. Under the heading "News," triple-click the first sub heading "Our Global Company Selected as One of the Top 10 Consulting Companies".
	f. Choose **Insert→Bookmark.**
	g. In the **Bookmark** dialog box, in the **Bookmark name** text box, type *One of the top 10 companies* and click **OK.**

2. Add links to the bookmarked sections.

a. Scroll up and then on the second line, double-click the text "Our Global Company selected as one of the top 10 consulting companies" to select it.

b. Choose **Insert→Hyperlink.**

c. If necessary, in the **Insert Hyperlink** dialog box, verify that the **Existing File or Web Page** button is selected.

d. In the **Insert Hyperlink** dialog box, click **Bookmark.**

e. In the **Select Place in Document** dialog box, click the **One of the top 10 companies** bookmark and then click **OK.**

f. In the **Insert Hyperlink** dialog box, click **OK.**

g. Scroll down and, double-click the text "Top" to select it.

h. Choose **Insert→Hyperlink.**

i. In the **Insert Hyperlink** dialog box, click **Bookmark.**

j. In the **Select Place in Document** dialog box, select the **Top** bookmark and click **OK.**

k. In the **Insert Hyperlink** dialog box, click **OK.**

l. Save newsrelease.aspx.

3. Test the bookmark link.

   a. Click the **Preview in Browser** button.

   b. Click the "Our Global Company selected as one of the top 10 consulting companies" hyperlink.

   c. Observe that the "Our Global Company Selected as One of the Top 10 Consulting Companies" section is displayed.

   d. Click the "Top" hyperlink.

   e. Observe that you are returned to the top of the page.

   f. Close the browser window.

   g. Close newsrelease.aspx.

TOPIC D
Add an Interactive Button

You added hyperlinks and bookmarks to navigate between web pages. Navigation can be made more interesting by adding interactivity to them. In this topic, you will add interactive buttons.

Sometimes, your website might be following a specific theme and a simple text link may not fit in the scheme of things. You may prefer to add a button that performs the same function as a link, yet one that is more visually appealing and that blends with the web page theme. With SharePoint Designer, you can add interactive buttons to your web pages easily.

Interactive Buttons

An *interactive button* is a button with link functionality that not only changes its appearance based on the user's mouse movement over the button but also links to another page. By default, an interactive button contains three states: original, hovered, and pressed. When you add an interactive button to a web page, SharePoint Designer creates three button images for each button state. You can save these button images onto the website using the **Save Embedded Files** dialog box.

The Interactive Buttons Dialog Box

The **Interactive Buttons** dialog box contains the **Button, Font,** and **Image** tabs from which you can choose the desired options to add and modify the interactive buttons. You can also preview the changes as you format the text or modify the button images.

Tab	Description
Button	Contains options to set the properties of an interactive button.
	• **Preview: Move cursor over button and click for sample:** Enables you to preview the selected image.
	• **Buttons:** Select a button type from the list of buttons.
	• **Text:** Specify the text that will be displayed on the button.
	• **Link:** Specify the path to the web page that needs to be opened when the button is clicked.

Tab	Description
Font	Contains options to format the text that is displayed on the button. • **Preview: Move cursor over button and click for sample:** Preview the button image while formatting the button text. • **Font:** Specify the font that can be applied to the button text. • **Font Style:** Specify font styles that you want to be applied to the button text. • **Size:** Specify the font size. • **Original Font Color, Hovered Font Color,** and **Pressed Font Color:** Set the font color for each of the button states. • **Horizontal Alignment** and **Vertical Alignment:** Specify the horizontal and vertical alignment of the text on the button image.
Image	Provides options to modify the button image. • **Width** and **Height:** Set the width and height of a button image. • **Create hover image** and **Create pressed image:** Manage the display of the button images that appear when you hover or press the mouse button on the button image. • **Preload button images:** Enable or disable the preloading images feature. • **Make the button a JPEG image and use this background:** Change the button to a JPEG image. You can also add a background color for the button image. • **Make the button a GIF image and use a transparent background:** Allows you to change the button to a GIF image with a transparent background.

How to Add an Interactive Button

Procedure Reference: Add an Interactive Button to a Web Page

To add an interactive button to a web page:

1. Open the desired web page.
2. Place the insertion point in the desired location and choose **Insert→Interactive Button.**
3. In the **Interactive Buttons** dialog box, in the **Buttons** list box, select the desired button.
4. In the **Text** text box, type the desired text that will be displayed on the button.
5. Link the button to a web page.
   - In the **Link** text box, type the path to the web page.
   - Or, click **Browse** and, in the **Edit Hyperlink** dialog box, navigate to the required location and open the desired page.
6. Save the page.
7. Save the button images in the desired folder.
8. Preview the page.

Procedure Reference: Modify Interactive Buttons

To modify an interactive button:

1. Open the web page that contains an interactive button.
2. Display the **Interactive Buttons** dialog box.
   - Select the button and choose **Insert→Interactive Button.**
   - From the button context menu, choose **Button Properties.**
   - Or, double-click the interactive button.
3. If necessary, in the **Interactive Buttons** dialog box, select the **Font** tab and format the font.
4. If necessary, select the **Image** tab and modify the button image.
5. Click **OK.**
6. If necessary, save the page.
7. If necessary, save the button images in the desired folder.
8. If necessary, preview the page.

ACTIVITY 5-6

Adding Interactive Buttons

Scenario:

A few of your colleagues have reviewed your website. They found that the overall design of the web pages is pleasing and attractive. One of your colleagues suggests that adding an interactive button to the web pages would make them livelier and more appealing. You find that SharePoint Designer has prebuilt interactive buttons that will enable you to add interactive buttons to the web pages easily.

What You Do	How You Do It
1. Display the **Interactive Buttons** dialog box.	a. In the **Folder List** task pane, double-click the **steve.aspx** page.
	b. Scroll down, place the insertion point at the end of the paragraph, and press **Enter.**
	role in meeting the marketing needs of the newly started Computing Services Department.
	c. Choose **Insert→Interactive Button.**
2. Add a functionality to the interactive button.	a. In the **Interactive Buttons** dialog box, in the **Buttons** list box, scroll down and select **Embossed Rectangle 1.**
	b. In the **Text** text box, triple-click and type *<< Back*
	c. Click **Browse** and, in the **Edit Hyperlink** dialog box, scroll down, select **employeecorner.aspx,** and click **OK** to link the interactive button to the **employeecorner.aspx** page.

3.	Modify the interactive button.	a.	In the **Interactive Buttons** dialog box, select the **Font** tab.
		b.	On the **Font** tab, in the **Font** list box, scroll down and select **Trebuchet MS.**
		c.	Select the **Image** tab.
		d.	On the **Image** tab, uncheck the **Maintain proportions** check box and in the **Width** text box, double-click and type *70*
		e.	Click **OK.**
4.	Save the page and the button images.	a.	Save steve.aspx.
		b.	In the **Save Embedded Files** dialog box, click **Change Folder** and in the **Change Folder** dialog box, select **images** and click **OK.**
		c.	In the **Save Embedded Files** dialog box, click **OK.**
5.	Test the **steve.aspx** page.	a.	Click the **Preview in Browser** button.
		b.	On the **steve.aspx.** page, scroll down and click the **<< Back** button.
		c.	Close the browser window.
		d.	Close steve.aspx.

TOPIC E
Open a Page in a New Browser Window

You are now familiar with adding interactive buttons to your web pages. There may be times when you may want to link one page to another, which needs to open in a new browser window. In this topic, you will open a page in a new browser window.

Sometimes, users might want to cross check the contents of multiple pages at the same time. In such a scenario, web pages opening up in the same browser window may not be helpful. Navigating back and forth between pages can be tedious and the user might lose interest. The Open Browser Window feature in SharePoint Designer enables you to open web pages in a separate browser window.

Behaviors

A *behavior* is a combination of an event and a resulting action. It helps you to add interactivity to the websites you create. You can add any number of behaviors to an element on a web page. When multiple behaviors with the same event are added to an element, the behavior that was added first will be performed foremost.

The Behaviors Task Pane

The **Behaviors** task pane enables you to add and edit behaviors on a web page or a selected element on the page. It displays all the behaviors that can be applied to a selected element.

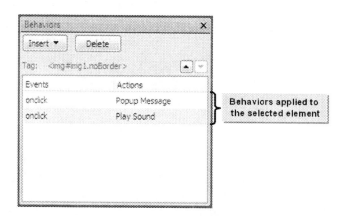

Figure 5-3: The options in the Behaviors task pane.

The following table lists the options in the **Behaviors** task pane.

Option	Description
The **Insert** drop-down list	Displays a list of behaviors that can be added to the selected element on the web page.
The **Delete** button	Enables you to delete the selected behavior in the **Behaviors** task pane.

Option	Description
The **Tag** option	Displays the tag corresponding to the selected element. When no elements are selected on a web page, the behaviors will be added to the default tag, **<body>.**
The **Move Up** and **Move Down** buttons	Enables you to move the selected behavior up or down.
The **Events** column	Lists the events that are associated with the behaviors that are added to the selected element on a page. When you place the mouse pointer over a behavior, it displays a drop-down list containing the events that can be added to the behavior.
The **Actions** column	Lists the behaviors' actions that need to be performed, when triggered by an event.

Types of Behaviors

SharePoint Designer enables you to add different types of behaviors for a selected element on the web page.

The following table lists some of the commonly used behaviors.

Behavior	Enables You To
Go To URL	Display the **Go To URL** dialog box where you can specify the URL of the page you want to open.
Open Browser Window	Open a page in a new browser window. This option opens the **Open Browser Window** dialog box, where you can specify the URL of the destination page, width and height of the new window, and set attributes such as adding a navigation bar and a menu bar.
Play Sound	Display the **Play Sound** dialog box, where you can specify an audio file that you want to insert on the web page.
Set Text	Set text for a selected element, so that when a specific event is performed on the element, the specified text will be displayed on the browser's status bar.
Swap Image	Swap an image with another, when the specific event is performed on the original image.
Check Browser	Display the **Check Browser** dialog box, where you can specify a browser type and the page that needs to be displayed for users using the selected browser. The dialog box also contains options for specifying a different page to be displayed for users who use other browser types.

Behavior	Enables You To
Jump Menu	Create a drop-down menu with multiple list items from which you can choose the desired option. You can also set a size for the menu. You can link each list item to a web page, which will be opened when the respective item is selected.

Additional Types of Behaviors

Some of the additional behaviors that you can add to your web page using SharePoint Designer are listed in the following table.

Behavior	Enables You To
Call Script	Display the **Call Script** dialog box, where you can call or specify a javascript code.
Change Property	Change the properties of a selected element so that the element changes when an event is performed.
Change Property Restore	Restore the last set of changed element properties.
Check Plug-in	Display the **Check Plug-in** dialog box, where you can specify a plug-in and a link to the page that needs to be opened if the user uses the selected plug-in. You can also specify a different page to be displayed for users who use other plug-ins.
Jump Menu Go	Add the Go button functionality for the jump menu.
Popup Message	Create a pop-up message that pops up when the specific action is triggered.
Preload Images	Load the alternate rollover images once the page loads. This enables you to swap the rollover images faster.
Swap Image Restore	Restore to the original image once the mouse pointer is moved out of the image.

Events

An event is a part of a behavior that triggers the browser to perform an action. When you add behaviors to a web page using SharePoint Designer, the default event is created along with the action. You can then change the default event by choosing a new event from the event's drop-down list. You can also specify different events for a single element.

Types of Events

There are different types of events that enable you to make your website interactive. The following table lists some of the commonly used event types.

Event	Triggers An Action
onclick	When a user performs a click action.
ondbclick	When a user performs a double-click action.
onkeypress	When a user presses a key on the keyboard.
onload	When the page is loaded.
onmouseover	When a user points the mouse pointer over the element.
onmousedown	When the mouse button is held down.
onmouseup	When the mouse button is pressed and then released.

Additional Event Types

Some of the additional events that you can add to your web page using SharePoint Designer are listed in the following table.

Events	Triggers An Action
onkeydown	When the user holds down a key.
onkeyup	When a key is pressed and then released.
onmousemove	When the mouse pointer is moved over an element.
onmouseout	When the mouse pointer is moved away from an element.
onunload	When the user exits a page.

The Open Browser Window Dialog Box

The **Open Browser Window** dialog box enables you to specify the URL of a web page and open the web page in a new browser window.

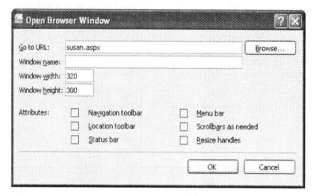

Figure 5-4: The options in the Open Browser Window dialog box.

Option	Enables You To
Go to URL	Link to a page that you want to open in a new browser window.
Window name	Set the new page to be opened in a different frame on the same page.
Window width	Specify the width of the window.
Window height	Specify the height of the window.
Attributes	Set the attributes for the new browser window.
	• **Navigation toolbar:** Display the navigation toolbar in the browser window.
	• **Location toolbar:** Display the location toolbar in the browser window.
	• **Status bar:** Display the status bar in the browser window.
	• **Menu bar:** Display the menu bar in the browser window.
	• **Scrollbars as needed:** Display scroll bars in the browser window if the content cannot be displayed in the specified window size.
	• **Resize handles:** Display the resize handles to resize the browser window.

The CSS Properties Task Pane

The *CSS Properties task pane* is a context-sensitive task pane that enables you to modify the CSS properties of the selected element. It contains two sections: **Applied Rules** and **CSS Properties.** The **Applied Rules** section contains selectors that are applied to the selected item. When a mouse pointer is placed over a selector, it displays all the CSS rules applied to the selector. The **CSS Properties** section lists all the properties that are applied to the specific selector. The buttons at the top of the task pane enable you to change the way the properties are listed.

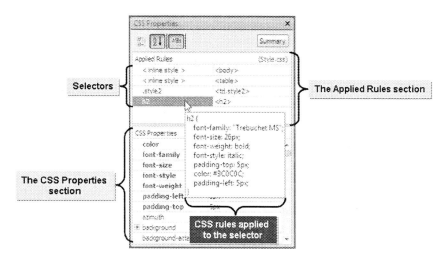

Figure 5-5: The options in the CSS Properties task pane.

How to Add a Behavior

Procedure Reference: Open a Web Page in a New Browser Window

To open a web page in a new browser window:

1. Open the desired web page.

2. Display the **Behaviors** task pane.

3. If desired, on the web page, select the desired web page element for which the behavior needs to be added.

 If no specific element on a web page is selected, the behavior, by default, will be added to the whole page—the <body> tag.

4. In the **Behaviors** task pane, from the **Insert** drop-down list, select **Open Browser Window.**

5. In the **Open Browser Window** dialog box, click **Browse.**

6. In the **Edit Hyperlink** dialog box, navigate to the required folder and open the desired web page.

7. If necessary, in the **Window width** and **Window height** text box, type the desired width and height for the browser window.

8. If necessary, in the **Attributes** section, set the desired attributes.

9. Click **OK.**

10. If necessary, in the **CSS Properties** task pane, in the **Layout** section, in the **pointer** drop-down list, select the desired pointer option.

11. If necessary, in the **Layout** section, in the **cursor** text box, click and type *pointer* and then press **Enter** to change the mouse pointer to a hand symbol when placed over the image.

12. If necessary, save and preview the page.

ACTIVITY 5-7

Opening a Page in a New Browser Window

Scenario:

The HR employees web page contains photographs of all the HR employees. You want to ensure that while the users view the details about each employee in a separate window, the main window remains open.

Your web designer has provided you with larger images, which are of 325 pixels high and 316 pixels wide, of the employees. You decide to set the same size for the new browser window, in order to avoid empty space around the photographs.

What You Do	How You Do It
1. Display the **Open Browser Window** dialog box.	a. In the **Folder List** task pane, double-click the **hremployees.aspx** page.
	b. On the **hremployees.aspx** page, select the first photograph.
	c. Choose **Task Panes→Behaviors** to display the **Behaviors** task pane.
	d. In the **Behaviors** task pane, from the **Insert** drop-down list, select **Open Browser Window.**
2. Specify the properties of the browser window.	a. In the **Open Browser Window** dialog box, click **Browse.**
	b. In the **Edit Hyperlink** dialog box, scroll down, select **maria.aspx,** and click **OK.**
	c. In the **Window name** text box, click and type *OGC*
	d. In the **Window width** text box, double-click and type *325*
	e. In the **Window height** text box, double-click and type *316*
	f. Click **OK.**
	g. Similarly, add the **Open Browser Window** behavior for the rest of the images on the page.

3. Change the cursor property.

a. Choose **Task Panes→CSS Properties** to display the **CSS Properties** task pane.

b. In the **CSS Properties** task pane, scroll down to view the **Layout** section.

c. In the **Layout** section, in the **cursor** text box, click and type *pointer* and then press **Enter** to change the mouse pointer to a hand symbol when placed over the image.

d. Close the **CSS Properties** and the **Behaviors** task panes.

e. Save hremployees.aspx.

f. In the **Save Embedded Files** dialog box, click **OK.**

4. Test the page.

a. Click the **Preview in Browser** button.

b. On the **hremployees.aspx** page, click the first image.

c. Observe that the **maria.aspx** page opens in a new browser window.

d. Close the browser windows.

e. Close hremployees.aspx and style.css.

Lesson 5 Follow-up

In this lesson, you used hyperlinks and bookmarks to connect the pages of your website. Linking web pages enables the site users to access the linked web pages instantaneously. You also used behaviors and interactive buttons that makes navigation through the site interesting.

1. **Discuss a list of scenarios where hotspots can come in handy on your websites.**

2. **What are the different interactive and dynamic features that you have seen in web pages and how do they add value to the website?**

6 | Adding SharePoint Components to the Site

Lesson Time: 1 hour(s)

Lesson Objectives:

In this lesson, you will add SharePoint components to the site.

You will:

- Add a list and library.
- Work with Web Parts.
- Add a link bar.
- Add more navigation links to the site.

Introduction

So far you have enhanced your web pages using CSS- and HTML-based functionality. SharePoint Designer provides unique SharePoint components that enhance the functionality and facilitate collaboration and easy navigation among the users of your SharePoint sites. In this lesson, you will add SharePoint components to a website.

Building an intranet site that provides a collaborative workspace and easy navigation has always been a tough task. You might need to expend a lot of time and effort to build heavy applications and integrate them onto your web pages. But that's a thing of the past. With SharePoint designer, you can use the prebuilt SharePoint components to add and customize functionality that supports the specific functional needs of the organization with ease.

TOPIC A
Add Lists and Libraries to a Site

You have created a website and added content and interactive features to the web pages. Another advanced functionality that you can add to your site are the lists and libraries, which can be used for sharing information and collaborating with other users. In this topic, you will add lists and libraries to the site to centralize the information for site users.

One of the most challenging aspects of working as a team is sharing of updated information. Each time the information changes, you have to get out the eraser or whiteout to change the hard copy, or make changes and resend an email message. Instead of going through that tedious process, you can add information to lists on your website where the information can be updated and it can be available for use by everyone. Similarly, managing files is also a tedious task. Files are often stored in numerous locations, including the network, individual hard drives, and removable media like thumb drives. With information in so many locations, it is easy to overlook important documents or waste valuable time creating a document that already exists. If you can both upload existing documents and create new documents in a SharePoint library, you will have one location for every file the team will need.

SharePoint Lists

Definition:

A SharePoint *list* is a content structure in a SharePoint site that contains a group of similar items, which can be shared among site users. When a list is added to a SharePoint site, a folder structure is created for the list, and it is displayed in the **Folder List** task pane. The folder contains four default web pages—**AllItems.aspx, DispForm.aspx, EditForm.aspx,** and **NewForm.aspx.** There are many types of lists that can be added using SharePoint Designer. Some of the list items are the announcements, the calendar, links, and tasks.

Example:

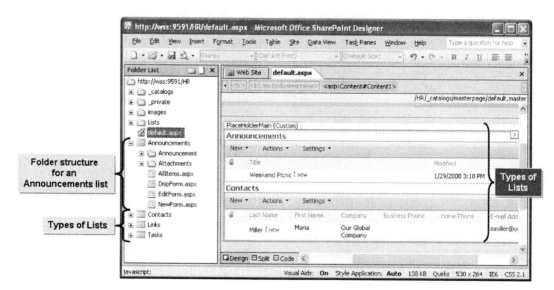

Types of Lists

There are several types of lists that can be added using SharePoint Designer.

Type	Description
Announcements	Contains short information items such as recent news or status updates.
Calendar	Keeps track of team meetings, deadlines, holidays, or other important events.
Contacts	Contains and manages information about individuals and groups, such as clients or vendors.
Custom Lists	A customized list wherein you can specify the number and type of columns that will appear in the list item.
Custom List in Datasheet View	A customized list wherein you can specify the number and type of columns. This customized list can be opened in a spreadsheet-like environment, which aids in managing data.
Discussion Board	Acts as an online forum, which will aid individuals to communicate through message posts.
Issue Tracking	Follows the progress of one or more issues.
Links	Displays the list of links from the Internet or your company intranet.
Project Tasks	Tracks the tasks for a project.
Tasks	Tracks the tasks that have been set for your team or a project.

SharePoint Document Libraries

Definition:

A SharePoint *document library* is a content structure in a SharePoint site; it contains files that can be shared among the site users. Like SharePoint lists, document libraries also contain a folder structure in the **Folder List** task pane with the default web pages in them. The default web pages are **AllItems.aspx, Combine.aspx, DispForm.aspx, EditForm.aspx, repair.aspx, Upload.aspx,** and **WebFldr.aspx.** A library may contain a single type of file such as a picture library, or it may contain multiple types of files including documents, spreadsheets, and presentations. There are separate libraries for pictures, forms, and wiki pages.

Example:

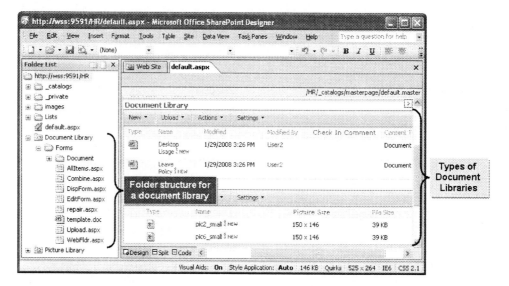

Types of Document Libraries

There are several types of document libraries that can be added using SharePoint Designer.

Type	Description
Document Library	Contains documents that can be shared among the site users.
Form Library	Contains XML (eXtensible Markup Language)-based forms such as invoices and expense reports used by programs such as Microsoft InfoPath.
Picture Library	Contains picture file types such as, .gif, and .jpg, that can be shared among the site users.
Wiki Page Library	Contains linked wiki pages and supports text, pictures, tables, and hyperlinks embedded in these pages.

How to Add a List and Document Library to a Site

Procedure Reference: Add a List or a Document Library to a Site

To add a list or a document library to a site:

1. Open a SharePoint site.

2. Choose **File→New→SharePoint Content.**

3. In the left pane, select **Lists** or **Document Libraries.**

4. In the middle pane, select the desired type of list or document library.

5. If necessary, in the **Options** section, specify a desired name for the list or document library item.

6. Click **OK.**

7. In the **Folder List** task pane, select the list or document library item added.

8. On the **Common** toolbar, click the **Preview in Browser** button to view the list or document library in the browser window.

 Each list or document library added to a SharePoint site gets stored on individual web pages.

ACTIVITY 6-1

Adding a List and Document Library to a Site

Before You Begin:

Ensure that the **Human Resources** subsite is kept open in SharePoint Designer.

Scenario:

For the Human Resources subsite, you want to have a centralized information repository, where you can assign tasks for your team members. You also want a document repository that your team members can use to share files.

What You Do	How You Do It
1. Add the **Tasks** list to the **Human Resources** subsite.	a. Choose **File→New→SharePoint Content**.
	b. If necessary, in the **New** dialog box, in the left pane, select **Lists**.
	c. In the middle pane, select **Tasks**.
	d. In the **Options** section, in the **Specify the name for the new list** text box, double-click the word "Tasks" and type *HR Tasks*
	e. Click **OK**.
2. Add a **Document Library** to the **Human Resources** subsite.	a. Choose **File→New→SharePoint Content**.
	b. In the left pane, select **Document Libraries**.
	c. Verify that in the middle pane, **Document Library** is selected.
	d. Click **OK**.

3. Preview the **HR Tasks** list and the **Document Library.**

   a. Choose **View→Refresh.**

   b. In the **Folder List** task pane, click **HR Tasks.**

   c. On the **Common** toolbar, click the **Preview in Browser** button.

   d. Observe that the **HR Tasks** list opens on a separate web page.

   e. Close the browser window.

   f. In the **Folder List** task pane, click **Document Library.**

   g. On the **Common** toolbar, click the **Preview in Browser** button.

   h. Observe that the **Document Library** opens as a separate web page.

   i. Close the browser window.

TOPIC B
Work with Web Parts

To create a centralized information system, you added lists and document libraries to your website. But these SharePoint components reside in their default web pages. To provide easy access for your users, you need to collate the lists and document libraries together and place them on a single page. In this topic, you will add Web Parts to your subsite, which will help you do just that.

A typical SharePoint site user might start his day checking out the tasks and announcements that are listed on the SharePoint site and then try to check out some documents to work on. The user will have to access each of these SharePoint components from different pages. SharePoint eliminates this disadvantage and offers us a solution that helps us collate all these SharePoint components onto one page.

Web Parts

A *Web Part* is the basic design element of a SharePoint site that contains information. The information contained within a Web Part can be an image, a list, or a document library. Web Parts can be easily added onto any web page by simply dragging them to the preferred position on the page.

All Web Parts are located in Web Part galleries and can be accessed from the **Web Parts** task pane. When a list or document library is added to a site, apart from getting listed in the **Folder List** task pane, it also gets added to the Web Part gallery.

Figure 6-1: *The Web Parts Task Pane listing the Web Parts.*

Examples of Web Parts

Some examples of items that can be contained in a Web Part are **Links, Discussion Board, Issue Tracking, Page Viewer,** and **Shared Documents.**

Web Part Zones

A *Web Part zone* is a container that contains one or more Web Parts. Web Part zones enable users to group and organize Web Parts. When Web Parts are placed in a Web Part zone, users can place them either horizontally or vertically. Also, Web Parts placed inside a Web Part zone can be customized by site users through the browser. The Web Parts that are not placed in a Web Part zone cannot be customized by site users through the browser. However, they can be customized using SharePoint Designer. This particular feature is useful when you do not want the end users to modify a Web Part.

 Web pages that contain Web Parts are referred to as Web Part pages.

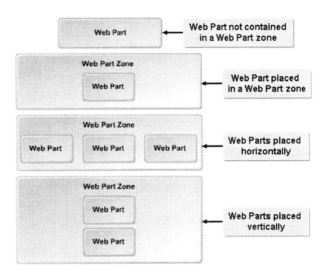

Figure 6-2: *Web Parts placed in a Web Part zone.*

The Web Parts Task Pane

The **Web Parts** task pane lists all the Web Parts available in different galleries. It provides you with various options that enable you to work with Web Parts.

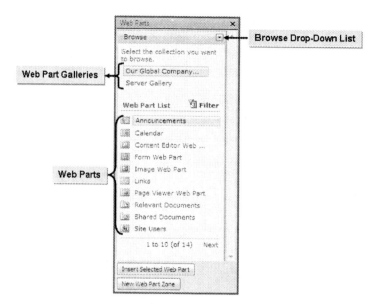

Figure 6-3: *The options in the Web Parts task pane.*

The following table lists the options available in the **Web Parts** task pane.

Option	Description
Browse drop-down list	Enables you to browse through the various Web Part galleries, import a Web Part from an external source, or search for Web Parts across the different galleries using the **Search** text box.
Web Part galleries	Lists the various collections of Web Parts available across the site.
Web Part List	Displays the Web Parts listed for the selected gallery.
Filter	Displays the **Show** drop-down list that allows you to change the category by which all the available Web Parts are displayed.
Insert Selected Web Part	Enables you to add Web Parts to a web page.
New Web Part Zone	Enables you to insert Web Part zones on a web page.

Default Web Parts in the Web Parts Task Pane

The following table lists the default Web Parts displayed in the Web Parts Task Pane.

Web Part	Enables You To
Content Editor Web Part	Add text and format it using the **Rich Text** Editor.

Web Part	Enables You To
Form Web Part	Connect to other Web Parts using simple form controls. It also enables you to filter a data column in another Web Part.
Image Web Part	Add and display pictures and photos.
Page Viewer Web Part	Display another file, folder, or a web page inside a Web Part.
Relevant Documents	Display documents that are relevant to a specific user.
Site Users	Display the names of the site users and groups.
User Tasks	Display the tasks assigned to a specific user.
XML Web Part	Display XML and XSL documents using the **XML Editor** and **XSL Editor.**

The Web Part Properties Dialog Box

The Web Part properties dialog box helps in customizing the Web Part to suit user preferences. It consists of different sections that enable you to configure the Web Part in the desired manner.

 The title of the Web Part properties dialog box corresponds to the name of the Web part.

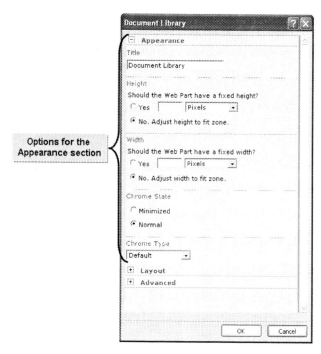

Figure 6-4: The options in the Web Part Properties dialog box.

Section	Description
Appearance	Contains properties such as **Title, Height/Width,** and **Chrome State** that control the appearance of the Web Part.
Layout	Contains properties that enable you to specify whether the Web Part should be kept open, closed, or hidden on the web page.
Advanced	Contains properties that control the advanced characteristics of a Web Part. It enables you to specify whether the Web Part can be minimized, closed, or hidden by the end user. It also enables you to specify if a Web Part can be moved to a different Web Part zone.

The Appearance Section of the Web Part Properties Dialog Box

The following table lists the properties of the Web Part that can be customized in the **Appearance** section.

Properties	Enables You To
Title	Specify the title of the Web Part.
Height/Width	Specify the height and width of the Web Part.

Properties	Enables You To
Chrome State	Specify whether the Web Part should be maximized or only the Web Part title should appear, when the Web Part page is accessed by a user. By default, it is set to **Normal** so that the Web Part appears maximized on the web page.
Chrome Type	Specify whether the title and the border of the Web Part should be displayed along with the Web Part.

The Layout Section of the Web Part Properties Dialog Box

The following table lists the properties of the Web Part that can be customized in the **Layout** section.

Properties	Enables You To
Close the Web Part	Specify whether the Web Part should be kept open or closed on the web page.
Hidden	Specify whether the Web Part is visible or hidden when a user tries to access the Web Part page.

The Advanced Section of the Web Part Properties Dialog Box

The following table lists the properties of the Web Part that can be customized in the **Advanced** section.

Properties	Enables You To
Allow Minimize	Specify whether the Web Part should be kept minimized when a user tries to access the Web Part page.
Allow Close	Specify whether the Web Part is open or closed when a user tries to access the Web Part page.
Allow Hide	Specify whether the Web Part is visible or hidden when a user tries to access the Web Part page.
Allow Zone Change	Specify if a Web Part can be moved to a different Web Part zone.
Allow Connections	Specify whether the Web Part can be connected with other Web Parts.
Allow Editing in Personal View	Specify whether the user is permitted to modify the Web Part properties in his/her personal view.

Properties	Enables You To
Title URL	Specify the URL of the file corresponding to the Web Part that resides in the **Folder List** task pane.
Description	Specify the screen tip that will appear when you move the mouse pointer over the Web Part title.
Help URL	Specify the location of a help file that contains help information about the Web Part.
Help Mode	Specify how the help information about the Web Part is displayed on the browser window.
Catalog Icon Image URL	Specify the location of an image file that can be used as the Web Part icon.
Title Icon URL	Specify the location of an image file that can be used in the Web Part title bar.
Import Error Message	Specify an error message that will be displayed if there is a problem while importing the Web Part.

The Displayed Fields Dialog Box

The various options in the **Displayed Fields** dialog box are used to add fields to the Web Part or remove fields from the Web Part, and also to change the order in which the fields are displayed on the Web Part.

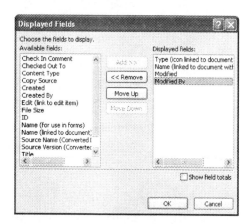

Figure 6-5: The various options in the Displayed Fields dialog box.

The following table describes the options available in the **Displayed Fields** dialog box.

Option	Description
Available fields	Displays the list of fields that can be added to the Web Part.

Option	Description
Displayed fields	Displays the list of fields already present on the Web Part.
Add/Remove buttons	Enables you to add or remove fields from the Web Part.
Move Up/ Move Down buttons	Enables you to change the order in which the fields are displayed on the Web Part.
Show field totals	Displays the total number of fields displayed in the Web Part.

How to Work with Web Parts

Procedure Reference: Insert a Web Part on a Web Page

To insert a Web Part on a web page:

1. Open the desired web page.
2. Choose **Task Panes→Web Parts** to open the **Web Parts** task pane.
3. If necessary, maximize the **Web Parts** task pane to view the entire **Web Parts** list.
4. If the web page is attached to a master page, in the editing window, place the mouse pointer in the content region, click the right arrow, and choose **Create Custom Content.**
5. Click on a desired location inside the content region.
6. In the **Web Parts** task pane, click **New Web Part Zone** to add a Web Part zone to the web page.
7. Choose the Web Part that you want to insert on the web page.
    -   Select a gallery from the gallery list, and choose the desired Web Part.
    -   Click **Filter,** and from the **Show** drop-down list, select the type of Web Part gallery to be displayed and choose the desired Web Part.
    -   Or, click **Next** or **Previous** to view the other Web Parts in the current Web Part gallery.
8. Place the Web Part on the web page.
    -   In the **Web Part** task pane, click **Insert Selected Web Part.**
    -   Or, from the **Web Part** task pane, drag the **Web Part** to the desired location on the web page.
9. On the **Common** toolbar, click the **Save** button.
10. If necessary, on the **Common** toolbar, click the **Preview in Browser** button to preview the page.

Procedure Reference: Customize a Web Part

To customize a Web Part:

1. In the editing window, select the desired Web Part.
2. Display the Web Part properties dialog box.
    -   On the Web Part, from the **List View Options** drop-down list, select **Web Part Properties.**
    -   Or, right-click the Web Part, and choose **Web Part Properties.**

3. Modify the Web Part.

- In the **Appearance** section of the **Web Part Properties** dialog box, choose the required settings to specify the title and dimensions of the Web Part.

- In the **Layout** section of the **Web Part Properties** dialog box, specify whether the Web Part will be visible, hidden, or closed when viewed in a browser.

- Or, in the **Advanced** section of the **Web Part Properties** dialog box, choose the required settings to set the advanced properties of the Web Part.

4. Click **OK.**

5. On the Web Part, from the **List View Options** drop-down list, select **Fields** to display the **Displayed Fields** dialog box.

 Almost all Web Parts contain different fields, except for Web Parts such as **Calendar**, which does not contain any fields.

6. Customize the fields in the Web Part.

- If necessary, in the **Displayed Fields** dialog box, in the **Available fields** list, select a desired field and click **Add** to add a field to the Web Part.

- If necessary, in the **Displayed Fields** dialog box, in the **Displayed fields** list, select a desired field and click **Remove** to remove a field from the Web Part.

- If necessary, click **Move Up** or **Move Down** to arrange the order in which the fields will be displayed on the Web Part.

7. In the **Displayed Fields** dialog box, click **OK.**

8. Save and preview the page.

ACTIVITY 6-2

Inserting a Web Part on a Web Page

Scenario:

You have added SharePoint lists and document libraries to the Human Resources subsite. But they appear on separate web pages. For ease of access for the users, you want to integrate them onto the home page of the Human Resources subsite.

What You Do	How You Do It
1. Insert a **Web Part Zone** on the home page of the **Human Resources** subsite.	a. In the **Folder List** task pane, double-click **default.aspx** to open the home page of the **Human Resources** subsite.
	b. Choose **Task Panes→Web Parts** to open the **Web Parts** task pane.
	c. In the editing window, click inside the second content region, click the right arrow next to it, and choose **Create Custom Content.**

	d. Click inside the **PlaceHolderMain (Custom)** content region.

	e. In the **Web Parts** task pane, click **New Web Part Zone.**

2.	Add the **HR Tasks** and the **Document Library** Web Part to the **default.aspx** page.	a.	In the **Web Parts** task pane, in the **Web Part List** section, select **HR Tasks.**
		b.	Click **Insert Selected Web Part** to add the **HR Tasks** Web Part to the **default.aspx** page.
		c.	In the editing window, scroll down and from the **Web Parts** task pane, drag the **Document Library** Web Part below the **HR Tasks** list Web Part inside the Web part zone.

3.	Save and preview the page.	a.	Click the **Save** button.
		b.	Click the **Preview in Browser** button to preview the page.
		c.	Observe that **HR Tasks and Document Library** are displayed on the home page.

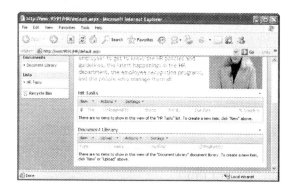

		d.	Close the browser window.

ACTIVITY 6-3
Customizing a Web Part

Scenario:
You had asked some of the members of the Human Resources team to test the usability of the **Document Library** Web Part, that has been added to their subsite. They suggest some changes that will further enhance the functionality of the Web Part. They suggest you to change the title of the Web Part to match that of the subsite. Also, they feel that some extra fields need to be added, and some redundant fields deleted. Finally, they also suggest you to make sure that users will not be able to close the **Document Library** Web Part.

What You Do	How You Do It
1. Change the title of the **Document Library** Web Part.	a. Verify that in the editing window, the **Document Library** Web Part is selected.
	b. Move the mouse pointer over the **List View Options** and from the drop-down list that appears, select **Web Part Properties.**

	c. In the **Appearance** section of the **Web Part Properties** dialog box, in the **Title** text box, select the words "Document Library", and type *HR Document Library*
2. Restrict the users from closing the Web Part.	a. In the **Document Library** dialog box, expand the **Advanced** section.
	b. Scroll down, and uncheck the **Allow Close** check box.
	c. In the **Document Library** dialog box, click **OK.**
	d. If necessary, in the **Auto Complete** dialog box, click **No.**

3.	Add the **Check In Comment** field and remove the **Modified** field from the **Document Library** Web Part.	a.	Move the mouse pointer over the **List View Options** and from the drop-down list that appears, select **Fields** to display the **Displayed Fields** dialog box.
		b.	Verify that, in the **Displayed Fields** dialog box, in the **Available fields** list box, the **Check In Comment** field is selected, and click **Add.**
		c.	In the **Displayed fields** list box, select **Modified** and click **Remove.**
		d.	Click **OK.**
4.	Save and preview the Web Part page.	a.	Click the **Save** button.
		b.	Click the **Preview in Browser** button to preview the page.
		c.	Observe that the **Check In Comment** field has been added, and the **Modified** field has been removed from the **HR Document Library** Web Part.

		d.	If necessary, in the browser window, scroll to the right and click **HR Tasks Web Part Menu.**
		e.	Observe that **HR Tasks Web Part Menu** has an option to close the **HR Tasks** Web Part.
		f.	Click anywhere outside the **HR Tasks Web Part Menu** to deselect the menu.
		g.	In the browser window, click **HR Documents Web Part Menu.**

h. Observe that **HR Documents Web Part Menu** does not have an option to close the **HR Documents** Web Part.

i. Click anywhere on the blue area to deselect the **HR Documents Web Part Menu** menu.

j. Close the browser window.

TOPIC C
Add a Link Bar

[handwritten: Do Not Do This.]

You have added Web Parts to your web pages. Another functional aspect that needs to be taken care of when developing a site is the site navigation. In this topic, you will add the **Link Bar** web component that will help users browse through the different pages of the site.

Just as you rely on the table of contents and index to find information in a reference book, users of your site rely on navigation components to find the information they need. By providing a navigation system on your website, you give users easy access to the information they seek.

Link Bars

[handwritten: Messes up links on Master Page]

A *link bar* is a collection of hyperlinks arranged vertically or horizontally on the web page and it is used to provide a navigation system for a site. By adding a link bar to the master page of a site, you can update the links across the whole site automatically.

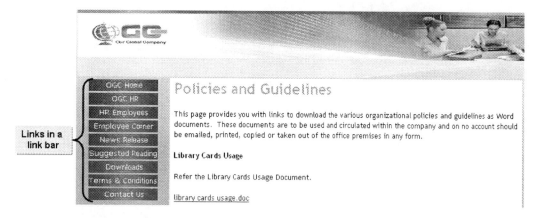

Figure 6-6: *Link bars in SharePoint Designer.*

The Insert Web Component Dialog Box

The **Insert Web Component** dialog box helps in adding a range of prebuilt features to the SharePoint site. Some of the features that can be added are hit counters that calculate the number of visitors to a site, photo galleries that store images, and link bars that provide a navigation structure for the site. Based on the web component we select from the **Component type** list box, the options in the right pane change. The **Find components on the web** link enables you to add web components available on the web.

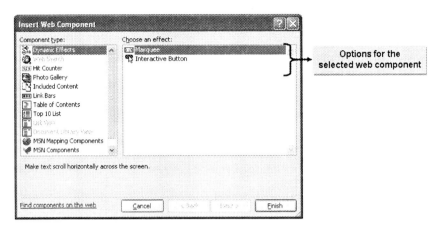

Figure 6-7: *The components in the Insert Web Component dialog box.*

The Link Bars Web Component

The **Link Bars** web component is one of the components that can be added to the SharePoint site using the **Insert Web Component** dialog box. This component aids in creating buttons that link to different web pages. It also offers you an option to choose the style or theme of the link bars from a list of default themes.

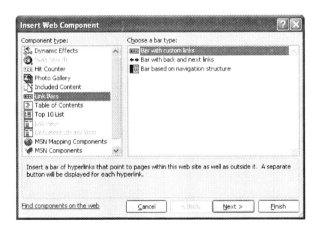

Figure 6-8: *The options in the Link Bars web component.*

The **Link Bar** web component offers you three options: **Bar with custom links, Bar with back and next links,** and **Bar based on navigation structure.**

Option	Enables You To
Bar with custom links	Add a list of links, organized either horizontally or vertically, that point to the pages in the website or points to some external links.
Bar with back and next links	Add links for pages that occur in a sequential order in your website.

Option	Enables You To
Bar based on navigation structure	Add a link bar based on the navigation structure of the site.

The Link Bar Properties Dialog Box

The **Link Bar Properties** dialog box helps to add more links to the link bar. This dialog box consists of two tabs: **General** and **Style.**

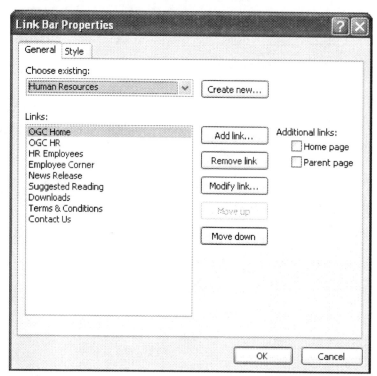

Figure 6-9: The options on the General tab of the Link Bar Properties dialog box.

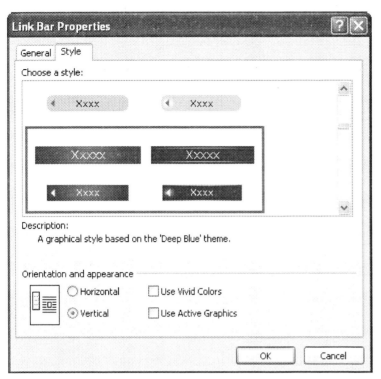

Figure 6-10: The options on the Style tab of the Link Bar Properties dialog box.

The following table lists the options displayed in the **Link Bar Properties** dialog box.

Tab	Description
General	The **General** tab provides you with options to modify the links in the link bar.
	● **Create new:** Enables you to create a new link bar.
	● **Add link:** Enables you to add new links to the link bar.
	● **Remove link:** Enables you to remove any unused links from the link bar.
	● **Modify link:** Enables you to rename a link. It also enables you to modify the properties of the link.
	● **Move up/Move down:** Enables you to change the order in which the links are displayed in the link bar. The **General** tab also consists of a **Choose existing** drop-down list, which enables you to choose from any existing link bars. The **Links** list box on the **General** tab displays the links that have been added for the chosen link bar.

Tab	Description
Style	Allows you to change the theme of the buttons in the link bar. It also provides you with options to choose the orientation and appearance of the link bars.

How to Add a Link Bar

Procedure Reference: Add a Link Bar

To add a link bar:

1. Open the desired website.
2. Open the master page of the site.
   - In the **Folder List** task pane, double-click the desired master page.
   - Or, in the **Web Site** pane, double-click the desired master page.
3. Place the insertion point where the link bar needs to be added.
4. Choose **Insert→Web Component** to open the **Insert Web Component** dialog box.
5. In the **Component type** list, select **Link Bars.**
6. In the **Choose a bar type** list, verify that **Bar with custom links** is selected and click **Next.**
7. In the **Insert Web Component** dialog box, click **Next.**
8. In the **Choose a bar style** list, select the desired style for the link bar and click **Next.**
9. In the **Choose an orientation** list, select an option to arrange the links either horizontally or vertically and click **Finish.**
10. In the **Create New Link Bar** dialog box, in the **Name** text box, specify the desired name for the link bar and click **OK.**
11. In the **Link Bar Properties** dialog box, in the **Additional links** section, check the **Home page** and **Parent page** check boxes and click **OK** to add links to the home page of the site.

Procedure Reference: Add Links to the Link Bar

To add links to the link bar:

1. In the **Design** view, right-click the link bar, and choose **Link Bar Properties** to open the **Link Bar Properties** dialog box.
2. In the **Link Bar Properties** dialog box, click **Add link** to add a link to the link bar.
3. In the **Add to Link Bar** dialog box, ensure that the **Existing File or Web Page** option is selected and then navigate to the desired web page.
4. In the **Add to Link Bar** dialog box, in the **Text to display** text box, specify a desired name for the link and click **OK.**
5. Repeat steps 2 to 4 to add more links to the link bar.
6. If necessary, in the **Links** list, select a link and click **Remove link** to remove the link from the link bar.
7. If necessary, in the **Links** list, select a link and click **Modify Link** to modify the link that appears in the link bar.

8. If necessary, in the **Links** list, select a link and click **Move up/Move down** to change the position of the links that appear in the link bar.

9. In the **Link Bar Properties** dialog box, click **OK.**

10. On the **Common** toolbar, click the **Save** button to save the master page.

11. If necessary, preview a web page that is attached to the master page.

* * END of DO NOT

DO THIS * *

Alternatively :- Drag aspx pages
onto layout. master page.

Ctrl + K (insets a hyperlink)
or Inset hyperlink.
or Inset Interactive Button

ACTIVITY 6-4

Adding a Link Bar

Scenario:

You plan to add a navigation structure for the Human Resources subsite. Your colleague suggests that you add links that will point to the organization's main site, and to the home page of the subsite. She also suggests a **Deep Blue** theme for the navigation structure, so that the navigation element would match the color theme of the subsite.

What You Do	How You Do It
1. Add a vertical link bar with the **Deep Blue** theme to the **layout.master** page of the Human Resources subsite.	a. In the **Folder List** task pane, double-click **layout.master**.
	b. In the left column of the master page, below the banner region, click below the OGC logo.

	c. Choose **Insert→Web Component** to open the **Insert Web Component** dialog box.
	d. In the **Component type** list box, select **Link Bars**.
	e. In the **Choose a bar type** list box, verify that **Bar with custom links** is selected and click **Next**.

f. In the **Choose a bar style** list box, scroll down and select the **Deep Blue** theme, which is the sixteenth theme in the list, and click **Next.**

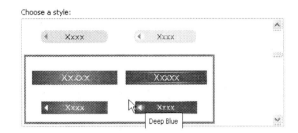

g. In the **Choose an orientation** list box, select the **Vertical** option to arrange the links in the link bar vertically and click **Finish.**

h. In the **Link Bar Properties** dialog box, click **Create new.**

i. In the **Create New Link Bar** dialog box, in the **Name** text box, type *Human Resources* and click **OK.**

2. Add a link that points to the home page of the OGC site.

a. In the **Link Bar Properties** dialog box, click **Add link.**

b. In the **Add to Link Bar** dialog box, in the **Address** text box, type *http://[sitename]*

c. In the **Text to display** text box, select the text and type *OGC Home*

d. In the **Add to Link Bar** dialog box, click **OK.**

3. Add a link that points to the home page of the Human Resources subsite.

a. In the **Link Bar Properties** dialog box, click **Add link.**

b. In the **Add to Link Bar** dialog box, scroll down and select **default.aspx.**

c. In the **Text to display** text box, select the text and type *OGC HR*

d. In the **Add to Link Bar** dialog box, click **OK.**

e. In the **Link Bar Properties** dialog box, click **OK.**

4. Test the page.

    a. On the **Common** toolbar, click the **Save** button.

    b. In the **Folder List** task pane, select **employeecorner.aspx.**

    c. Click the **Preview in Browser** button to preview the **Quick Launch** bar in the browser window.

    d. In the link bar, click the **OGC Home** link to navigate to the home page of the Human Resources subsite.

    e. Close the browser window.

    f. Close layout.master.

TOPIC D

Enhance the Navigation Structure

You have added a link bar to a site. SharePoint provides other aids that can enhance the navigation structure of a website by means of customizing the **Quick Launch** and the **Top Link** bar. In this topic, you will enhance the navigation structure.

In our personal computers, we often place the programs that we frequently use on our desktop as shortcut icons, for easy one-click access. Similarly, SharePoint Designer offers a solution that helps us access frequently used web pages or websites with ease.

The Navigation View

The *Navigation* view is an application pane that displays a graphical and hierarchical view of the site structure. The default components and pages in a SharePoint site get listed in the **Navigation** view by default. But, for the pages that are being added manually, you need to organize them in the **Navigation** view, to complete the navigation structure of the site. You can also assign unique display names to the pages displayed in the **Navigation** view.

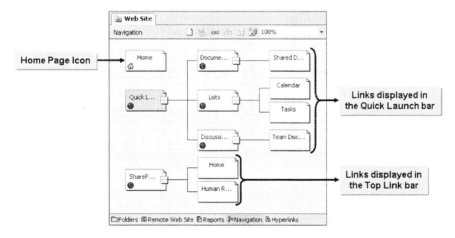

Figure 6-11: *The Navigation view in SharePoint Designer.*

The pages of a site are arranged under four page icons displayed in the **Navigation** view.

Page Icon	Description
Home	It represents the site's home page and is displayed toward the left in the **Navigation** view.
The **Quick Launch**bar	The links displayed in the **Quick Launch** bar of the site are organized under this page icon.
The **SharePoint Top Navigation**bar	The links displayed in the **Top Link** bar of the site are organized under this page icon.
The **Custom Link**bar	The links displayed in any available custom link bar of the site are organized under this page icon.

Navigation View Names

In the **Navigation** view, you can change the name of a page's icon. This change reflects only on the links in the **Quick Launch** bar, **Top Link** bar, or custom link bars. Changing the **Navigation** view name does not change the page's file name or title.

The Quick Launch Bar

The *Quick Launch bar* consists of a list of links displayed on the left side of a page in a SharePoint site. By default, the links in the **Quick Launch** bar are categorized as **Surveys, Pictures, Documents, Lists, Discussions, Sites,** and **People and Groups.** SharePoint Designer's **Navigation** view helps you add links to the **Quick Launch** bar, remove links from the **Quick Launch** bar, or rename the links in the **Quick Launch** bar. You can even change the order of the links in the **Quick Launch** bar.

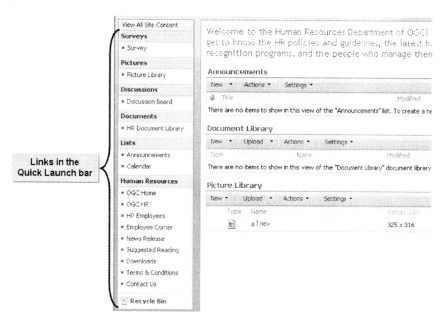

Figure 6-12: The Quick Launch bar in a SharePoint site.

The Top Link Bar

The *Top Link bar* is a collection of links, which appear as tabs at the top of the home page in a SharePoint site. Using SharePoint Designer's **Navigation** view, you can add links, which might be frequently accessed by users, to the **Top Link** bar.

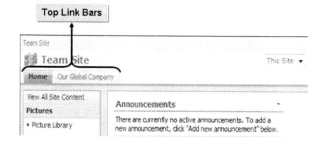

Figure 6-13: The Top Link bar in a SharePoint site.

How to Enhance the Navigation Structure

Procedure Reference: Customize the Quick Launch Bar

To customize the **Quick Launch** bar:

1. Open the desired website.
2. On the **Web Site** tab, select the **Navigation** view.
3. In the **Navigation** view, select the **Quick Launch Bar** link.
4. From the **Folder List** task pane, drag the desired web pages onto the **Navigation** view pane under the **Quick Launch Bar** link, to add more links to the **Quick Launch** bar.
5. Rename a link in the **Quick Launch** bar.
   a. Right-click the desired web page icon, and choose **Rename.**
   b. In the text box, type the desired name and press **Enter.**
6. If necessary, in the navigation view pane, reposition the web page icons to reorder the links in the **Quick Launch** bar.
7. In the **Navigation** view pane, select the home page icon and click the **Preview in Browser** button to preview the page.
8. If necessary, in the **Quick Launch** bar, click a desired link to test the page.

Procedure Reference: Add a Link to the Top Link Bar

To add a link to the **Top Link** bar:

1. Open the desired website.
2. On the **Web Site** tab, select the **Navigation** view.
3. In the **Navigation** pane, select the **SharePoint Top Navigation Bar** link.
4. Right-click the **SharePoint Navigation Bar** link, and choose **New→Page.**
5. If necessary, right-click the navigation pane and choose **Apply Changes** to refresh the page.
6. Right-click the web page icon and choose **Properties.**
7. In the **Edit Hyperlink** dialog box, navigate and select the desired web page.
8. Rename the link in the **Top Link** bar.
   a. Right-click the desired web page icon, and choose **Rename.**
   b. In the text box, type the desired name and press **Enter.**
9. If necessary, right-click the navigation pane and choose **Apply Changes** to refresh the page.
10. Preview the **Top Link** bar.
    a. In the navigation pane, select the **Home** icon.
    b. On the **Common** toolbar, click the **Preview in Browser** button.

ACTIVITY 6-5

Customizing the Quick Launch Bar

Before You Begin:
1. Close the **Data Source Details** task pane group.
2. Ensure that the **default.aspx** page of the Human Resources subsite is kept open.

Scenario:
While testing the usability of the Human Resources subsite, your team members are unable to navigate from the home page of the subsite to the other web pages. They suggest you to add links to the Quick Launch bar of the Human Resources home page, so that users are able to browse through all the web pages of the subsite.

What You Do	How You Do It
1. Add a link for the **Employee Corner** page in the **Quick Launch** bar of the Human Resources subsite.	a. On the **Common** toolbar, click the **Preview in Browser** button to view the **Quick Launch** bar of the Human Resources subsite.
	b. Observe that the **Quick Launch** bar does not have links to the pages of the Human Resources subsite. Close the browser window.

	c. In the editing window, select the **Web Site** tab and select the **Navigation** view.

d. From the **Folder List** task pane, drag the **hremployees.aspx** page onto the **Navigation** view pane under the **Human Resources** link to the right of the **OGC HR** page icon.

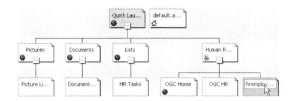

e. Right-click the **hremployees.aspx** web page icon, and choose **Rename.**

f. In the text box, type *HR Employees* and press **Enter.**

2. Add more links to the **Quick Launch** bar of the Human Resources subsite.

a. From the **Folder List** task pane, drag the **employeecorner.aspx** page onto the **Navigation** view pane under the **Human Resources** link to the right of the **HR Employees** page icon.

b. Right-click the **employeecorner.aspx** web page icon and choose **Rename.**

c. In the text box, type *Employee Corner* and press **Enter.**

d. Similarly, add links for the **newsrelease.aspx, suggestedreading.aspx, downloads.aspx, termsandconditions.aspx,** and **contactus.aspx** pages. Name them as News Release, Suggested Reading, Downloads, Terms & Conditions, and Contact Us respectively.

3. Test the **Quick Launch** bar.

a. In the **Navigation** view, select **default.aspx.**

b. On the **Common** toolbar, click the **Preview in Browser** button.

c. Observe that the **Quick Launch** bar on the left hand side of the page contains the links to the web pages of the Human Resources subsite.

View All Site Content

Documents

* HR Document Library

Lists

* HR Tasks

Human Resources

* OGC Home
* OGC HR
* HR Employees
* Employee Corner
* News Release
* Suggested Reading
* Downloads
* Terms & Conditions
* Contact Us

Recycle Bin

d. In the **Quick Launch** bar, click the **Employee Corner** link.

e. Observe that the link bar on the **employeecorner.aspx** page has also been updated with the links for all the web pages.

f. Close the browser window.

ACTIVITY 6-6

Adding a Link to the Top Link Bar

Scenario:

You've almost finalized the navigation structure for the site. As the final step, you decide to link the Human Resources subsite with the organization's top-level site so that all the pages of the main site and subsite are easily accessible.

What You Do	How You Do It
1. Add a new page to the **SharePoint Top Navigation Bar** link.	a. Choose **File→Open Site.**
	b. In the **Open Site** dialog box, in the **Site name** text box, type **http://[sitename]** and click **Open.**
	c. If necessary, in the **Connect to ogc** dialog box, type your login name and password and click **OK.**
	d. On the bottom of the **Web Site** tab, select the **Navigation** view.
	e. In the **Navigation** view, right-click the **SharePoint Top Navigation Bar** link and choose **New→Page.**
	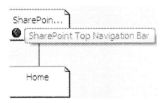
	f. Right-click the navigation pane and choose **Apply Changes** to refresh the page.

<table>
<tr>
<td>2.</td>
<td>Link the newly created page to the home page of the Human Resources subsite.</td>
<td>a.</td>
<td>Right-click the **Untitled 1** web page icon and choose **Properties.**</td>
</tr>
<tr>
<td></td>
<td></td>
<td>b.</td>
<td>In the **Edit Hyperlink** dialog box, in the **Current Folder** list box, double-click **Human Resources.**</td>
</tr>
<tr>
<td></td>
<td></td>
<td>c.</td>
<td>Scroll down, select **default.aspx,** and click **OK.**</td>
</tr>
<tr>
<td>3.</td>
<td>Rename the link in the **Top Link** bar.</td>
<td>a.</td>
<td>Right-click the **Human Resources/ default.aspx** web page icon and choose **Rename.**</td>
</tr>
<tr>
<td></td>
<td></td>
<td>b.</td>
<td>In the text box, type *Human Resources* and press **Enter.**</td>
</tr>
<tr>
<td>4.</td>
<td>Test the **Top Link** bar.</td>
<td>a.</td>
<td>In the navigation pane, select the **Home** page icon.</td>
</tr>
<tr>
<td></td>
<td></td>
<td>b.</td>
<td>Click the **Preview in Browser** button.</td>
</tr>
<tr>
<td></td>
<td></td>
<td>c.</td>
<td>Observe that the **Human Resources** tab has been added to the **Top Link** bar.</td>
</tr>
</table>

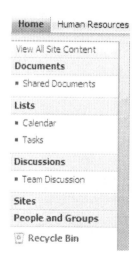

d. In the **Top Link** bar, click the **Human Resources** tab.

e. Close the browser window.

f. Choose **File→Exit.**

Lesson 6 Follow-up

In this lesson, you added lists, document libraries, and link bars. When shared information is organized into lists or libraries, everyone on the team can quickly locate and work with the information they need. Also, adding links and customizing the **Quick Launch** bar provide the site a proper navigation structure and enable users to navigate through a site with ease.

1. **In your environment, for what purpose will you use a Tasks list?**

2. **What are the fields that you might add to the Web Part you use, to suit your organizational requirements?**

3. **How will you design the navigation structure for your site using SharePoint Designer?**

7 | Automating Business Processes with Workflows

Lesson Time: 1 hour(s), 5 minutes

Lesson Objectives:

In this lesson, you will automate business processes with workflows.

You will:

- Create a workflow.
- Modify a workflow.

Introduction

You have added lists and libraries to your site. SharePoint Designer makes it possible to integrate all such SharePoint components seamlessly with your business processes and automate them. In this lesson, you will automate business processes with workflows.

Imagine a workflow, where a developer wants to send a document for review. This would involve uploading the document onto the SharePoint's document library and sending an email to the reviewer informing about the availability of the document. The reviewer on viewing the email, downloads the document from the SharePoint site, reviews it, and uploads it back to the site. Wouldn't it be easier if the developer just uploads the document onto the site and then leave the email notifications and other tasks to be performed by SharePoint? SharePoint Designer allows you to automate the processes by creating customized workflows without the need to write any code.

TOPIC A
Create a Workflow

You have added lists and library to the site. In a SharePoint site, list and libraries can be linked to a business process and can perform certain tasks automatically. In this topic, you will create a workflow.

Any organization has its own set of business processes, which define the workflow within an organization. It is quite a task to ensure that the workflow functions the way you want it to and includes tracking every stage of the task and keeping the concerned people informed of the status through emails and other manual ways. But, its all going to be a thing of the past. With SharePoint designer, you can create workflows that assign tasks to people, send email notifications, or even collect information from the required users, without the need for any manual intervention.

SharePoint Workflows

A SharePoint workflow comprises a series of tasks performed in succession to produce a final outcome. It determines the flow of tasks among users and helps organize and execute various activities that represent the work process. A workflow also tracks the history of all the tasks performed within it.

Workflow Locations

SharePoint workflows are based on the lists and libraries in a site. All workflows created with SharePoint Designer are stored in a folder called **Workflows,** which resides in the site's main folder and can be modified when necessary. Each workflow consists of their respective source files that are required for the workflow.

Workflow Source Files

The source files of a workflow are made up of the XOML (eXtensible Object Markup Language) and the ASPX pages. The default XOML pages include: the workflow markup page, workflow rules page (.xoml.rules), and the workflow configuration page (xoml.wfconfig.xml). The ASPX pages are created when custom tasks are created or when the initiation parameters are specified.

The Workflow Designer Wizard

The Workflow Designer wizard takes you through a series of steps to create and modify workflows. It provides options to define a new workflow and to specify the details for each step in a workflow.

Option	Allows You To
The define your new workflow page	Define a workflow. It contains several options: • The **Give a name to this workflow** text box: Enables you to add a name for the website. • The **What SharePoint list should this workflow be attached to** option: Enables you to select the SharePoint list to which the workflow should be attached. • The **Select workflow start options for items in Document Library** section: Contains the **Allow this workflow to be manually started from an item, Automatically start this workflow when a new item is created,** and the **Automatically start this workflow whenever an item is changed** options. You can select any or all of the these options for the workflow to be initiated. • The **Check Workflow** button: Enables you to check the workflow for errors. • The **Initiation** button: Enables you to display the **Workflow Initiation Parameters** dialog box, where you can create and modify the custom initiation parameters. This helps you to collect additional information from users when the workflow is manually initiated. • The **Variables** button: Enables you to display the **Workflow Local Variables** dialog box, where you can add and manage the workflow variables. • The **Cancel, Back, Next,** and **Finish** buttons: Enables you to cancel the changes made to the workflow, move between the two pages in the Workflow Designer wizard, and save the changes made to the workflow respectively.

Option	Allows You To
The specify details page	Specify the details for a workflow. It contains several options.
	• The **Step Name** text box: Enables you to add a name for a workflow step.
	• The **Specify details for [step name]** section: Provides you with the **Conditions** and **Actions** drop-down lists that enable you to specify the conditions and actions for a workflow step. It also contains the **Add 'Else If' Conditional Branch** link that enables you to specify an alternate action that needs to be performed when the previous condition is not satisfied.
	• The **Workflow Steps** section: Enables you to add a new workflow step using the **Add workflow step** link. It also lists the names of the steps in the workflow. By selecting the step names in this section, you can view the actions and conditions of the selected step.

Workflow Steps

A workflow created using SharePoint Designer can contain several steps. A step is nothing but a combination of actions and conditions. The first step is initiated when the event specified for the for workflow to be initiated is performed while the subsequent steps are initiated upon completion of the previous step.

The Custom Task Wizard

The **Custom Task Wizard** allows you to create a new custom task and it contains options to add a name and description for the task. You can also add custom form fields that you want the user to fill while performing the task.

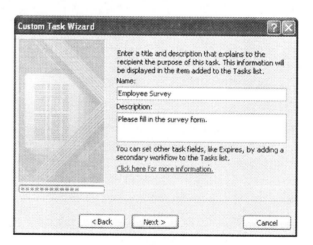

Figure 7-1: The Name and Description options in the Custom Task Wizard.

The Select Users Dialog Box

The **Select Users** dialog box allows you to select the users to whom you need to assign a task or send an email. It contains the **Type a Name or E-mail Address** text box, where you can type the name of the recipients. The **Or select from existing Users and Groups** list box lists the names of users from which you can select the users. The **Add** button allows you to add the users to the **Selected Users** list box and the **Remove** button allows you to remove the users from the **Selected Users** list box. The **Move Up** and **Move Down** buttons allow you to move the names in the **Selected Users** list box up and down, respectively.

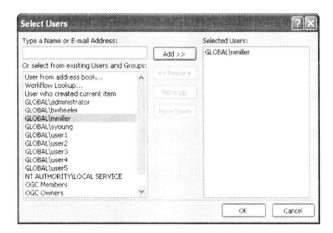

Figure 7-2: The options in the Select Users dialog box.

Workflow Components

Workflow components are the events, actions, and conditions and they instruct the workflow to follow a specific sequence for its successful completion.

Workflow Component	Description
Event	An event is a parameter that initiates a workflow. SharePoint Designer, by default provides you with three options to initiate a workflow. You can opt to start the workflow manually from an item, start the workflow when a new item is created, and start the workflow whenever an item is changed. You can also specify custom initiation parameters, if the workflow is set to be started manually from an item.

Workflow Component	Description
Action	An action is performed when triggered by an event. A workflow can contain more than one action. Some of the default actions that SharePoint Designer provides are: • **Send an Email:** Specify the name of the user you want to send the email to. You can also specify the subject and body content for the email. • **Assign a To-do Item:** Allows you to display the **Custom Task Wizard,** which enables you to create a new task. The action also contains the option to display the **Select Users** dialog box to assign the new task to a specific user.
Condition	Every action is associated with a condition. An action will be performed only when the specified conditions are met. Some of the default conditions that SharePoint Designer provides are: • **Compare [list/library name] field:** Specify the field and the value that need to be compared. The workflow is started when the specified field and the value matches with those of the list/library item. • **Title field contains keywords:** Specify a keyword that needs to be compared with the title field. The workflow is started when the title of the list/library item matches with the specified keyword. • **Created by a specific person:** Specify the name of a user. The workflow is started when the list/library item is created by the specified user.

The Define E-mail Message Dialog Box

The **Define E-mail Message** dialog box contains options using which you can add the user names and the message that need to be displayed in the email.

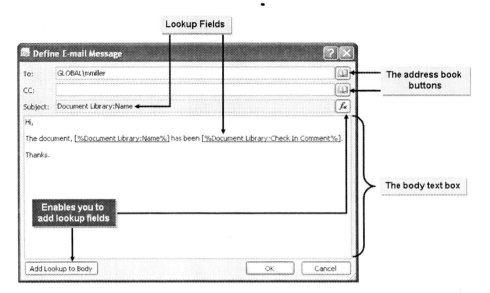

Figure 7-3: *The options in the Define E-mail Message dialog box.*

The following table lists the options in the **Define E-mail Message** dialog box.

Option	Description
The **To** text box	Enables you to type the email addresses of the users to whom you want to send the email.
The **CC** text box	Enables you to type the email addresses of the users to whom you want to send a copy of the email.
The **address book** button	Displays the **Select Users** dialog box, where you can select the names of users to whom you want to send the email or a copy of the email.
The **Subject** text box	Enables you to type the subject for the email.
The **body** text box	Enables you to type the body text for the email.
The **fx** and the **Add Lookup to Body** buttons	Displays the **Define Workflow Lookup** dialog box that allows you to select the data source and the field to perform the lookup on. The **Clear Lookup** button allows you to clear the lookup that you have created. The **fx** and the **Add Lookup to Body** buttons allow you to specify the lookup for the subject and the body respectively.

How to Create a Workflow

Procedure Reference: Create a Workflow

To create a workflow:

1. Open the website in which you want to create a workflow.

2. Ensure that the website contains the list or library on which the workflow should be based.

3. Choose **File→New→Workflow** to open the Workflow Designer wizard.

4. In the **Give a name to this workflow** text box, type the desired name.

5. From the **What SharePoint list should this workflow be attached to** drop-down list, select the necessary list or library item.

6. If necessary, in the **Select workflow start options for items in Announcements** section, select the desired options.

   - Check the **Allow this workflow to be manually started from an item** check box to initiate the workflow manually.

   - Check the **Automatically start this workflow when a new item is created** check box to initiate the workflow when a new item is created in the list or library on which the workflow is based.

   - Check the **Automatically start this workflow whenever an item is changed** check box to initiate the workflow when an item in the selected list or library is changed.

7. Click **Next**.

8. If necessary, in the **Step Name** text box, type a name for the step.

9. In the Specify details for '[step name]' section, from the **Conditions** drop-down list, select the desired option and specify the required values that will be checked for the workflow to be initiated.

   - Select the **Compare [list/library name] field** option and specify the values.

     - Click the **field** link and from the drop-down list, select the desired field.

     - Click the **equals** link and from the drop-down list, select the desired parameter.

     - Click the **value** link and in the text box, type the necessary keyword that needs to be compared with the specified field or, click **fx** and in the **Define Workflow Lookup** dialog box, from the **Source** drop-down list, select the required option from where the workflow should lookup for the field, and from the **Field** drop-down list, select the required field that has to be compared with the specified field. Click **OK.**

- Select the **Title field contains keywords** option to specify a keyword that needs to be compared with the title field by clicking the keywords link and typing the required keyword, or by opening the **Define Workflow Lookup** dialog box and specifying the required value.

- Select the **Created in a specific date span** option to specify the dates during which the elements in the list or library have been created by clicking the **date** links and typing the desired dates, or by opening the **Define Workflow Lookup** dialog box and specifying the required values.

- Select the **Modified in a specific date span** option to specify the dates during which the elements in the list or library have been modified by clicking the **date** links, or by opening the **Define Workflow Lookup** dialog box and specifying the required values.

- Select the **Created by a specific person** option to specify the name of the person who has modified the item in the list or library by clicking the specific **specific person** link, or by opening the **Define Workflow Lookup** dialog box and specifying the required values.

- Select the **Modified by a specific person** option to specify the name of the person who has modified the item in the list or library by clicking the specific **specific person** link, or by opening the **Define Workflow Lookup** dialog box and specifying the required values.

- Select the **The file size in a specific range kilobytes** option to specify the file size range of the items added to the list or library by clicking the **size** links, or by opening the **Define Workflow Lookup** dialog box and specifying the required values.

10. From the **Actions** drop-down list, select the desired action that needs to be performed once the specific condition is fulfilled.

- Select **Send an Email,** click the **this message** link, and in the **Define E-mail Message** dialog box, specify the required values.

  - In the **To** and **CC** text boxes, specify the required email addresses.

  - In the **Subject** text box, type the desired subject or click **fx** and in the **Define Workflow Lookup** dialog box, specify the required values that need to be displayed in the **Subject** text box.

  - In the body text box, type the required text or click **Add Lookup to Body** and in the **Define Workflow Lookup** dialog box, specify the required values that you want to appear as the body text.

- Select the **Assign a To-do Item** option and perform the necessary actions.

  a. Click the **a to-do item** link and in the **Custom Task Wizard,** click **Next** to specify a task, and in the **Name** text box, type the desired name for the task and then if necessary, in the **Description** text box, type a description. Click **Finish** to create a task.

  b. Click the **these users** link and in the **Select Users** dialog box, in the **Type a Name or E-mail Address** text box, type the desired email address and click **Add,** or in the **Or select from existing Users and Groups** list box, select the desired user names and click **Add.** Click **OK.**

11. If necessary, in the **Workflow Steps** section, click the **Add workflow step** link and perform steps 8 to 10 to add a new step to the workflow.

12. Click **Check Workflow** to check for any errors in the workflow.

13. If necessary, rectify the highlighted errors by adding the correct keywords or values.

14. Click **Finish.**

15. Test the workflow initiation.

- If you have chosen to manually start the workflow, if necessary, import a new document and from the document's drop down list, select **Workflows** and then in **Start a New Workflow** section, click the necessary workflow link and click **Start.** Check if the specified action such as sending an email, or assigning a task to a specific user has been performed.

- If you have chosen to automatically start the workflow when a new item is created, upload a new document and then check if the specified action has been performed.

- If you have chosen to automatically start the workflow whenever an item is changed, if necessary, upload a document and then modify the document. Check if the specified action has been performed.

16. Test the rest of the steps in the workflow by performing the necessary tasks and then checking if the specified action has been performed.

Pending Doc 1.b

any New Item ⟹ workflow ⟹ Bob

↓

Task (Central EE)

↓

Approve / Disapprove

← email Bob (Approval)
Move Item ⟹ Approved lib

↓ email Bob (nggood)
move Item from
pending l.b.

Whereever see ☒ = *On Object User Interface (OOUI)*

ACTIVITY 7-1
Creating an Approval Workflow

Data Files:

Samantha_Developer.doc

Setup:

In the HumanResources subsite, on the **Web Site** tab, switch to the **Folders** view.

Scenario:

Now that the website design and the structure are ready, the recruitment manager has come out with some requests. She wants certain tasks with respect to the resume management process to be automated.

1. When the HR executive posts the resume to the document library, a task needs to be assigned to the respective functional manager to review the document.

2. The functional manager, on viewing the task, checks out the document, reviews it, and places his comments while checking it back into the library. He also completes the task assigned to him.

3. Once the document is checked back into the library with the comment "Approved," the recruitment manager should receive an email asking him to schedule an interview.

Following are the roles involved and their email IDs.

- Susan Young (Human Resource Executive): syoung@ourglobalcompany.com
- Maria Miller (Recruitment Manager): mmiller@ourglobalcompany.com
- Bob Wheeler (Functional Manager): bwheeler@ourglobalcompany.com

What You Do	How You Do It
1. Define a new workflow.	a. Choose **File→New→Workflow** to open the Workflow Designer wizard.
	b. In the **Workflow Designer - Workflow 1** wizard, in the **Give a name to this workflow** text box, triple-click and type *Approval Workflow*
	c. Verify that from the **What SharePoint list should this workflow be attached to** drop-down list, the **Document Library** option is selected.
	d. Verify that the **Allow this workflow to be manually started from an item** check box is checked and click **Next.**

2. Specify the first step of the workflow.

a. In the **Specify details for 'Step 1'** section, from the **Conditions** drop-down list, select **Compare Document Library field.**

b. In the newly created condition, click the **field** link and in the drop-down list, scroll down and select **Name.**

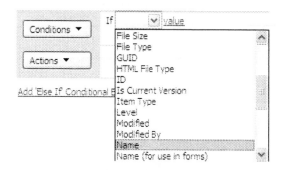

c. Click the **equals** link and from the drop-down list, select **contains.**

d. Click the **value** link and in the text box, type *Developer*

Keywords or values, in workflows are case sensitive. Ensure that you give the same name you specified in the value text box for the workflow to be initiated.

e. From the **Actions** drop-down list, select **Assign a To-do Item.**

f. In the newly created action, click the **a to-do item** link.

g. In the **Custom Task Wizard,** click **Next** to create a new task.

h. In the **Name** text box, type *Resume Verification* and press **Tab.**

i. In the **Description** text box, type *Please verify the resume.* and click **Finish** to complete the task creation process.

j. Click the **these users** link.

k. In the **Select Users** dialog box, in the **Or select from existing Users and Groups** list box, select **GLOBAL\bwheeler** and click **Add.**

l. Click **OK.**

3. Specify the second step of the workflow.

a. In the **Workflow Steps** section, click the **Add workflow step** link.

b. From the **Conditions** drop-down list, select **Compare Document Library field.**

c. In the newly created condition, click the **field** link and from the drop-down list, select **Check In Comment.**

d. Click the **equals** link and from the drop-down list, select **contains.**

e. Click the **value** link and in the text box, type *Approved*

f. From the **Actions** drop-down list, select the **Send an Email** action.

g. In the newly created action, click the **this message** link.

h. In the **Define E-mail Message** dialog box, next to the **To** text box, click the address book button.

i. In the **Select Users** dialog box, in the **Or select from existing Users and Groups** list box, select **GLOBAL\mmiller,** click **Add,** and then click **OK.**

j. Next to the **Subject** text box, click **fx.**

k. In the **Define Workflow Lookup** dialog box, in the **Field** drop-down list, scroll down and select **Name.**

l. Click **OK.**

m. Click in the body text box and type *Hi, The resume,* and then press the **Spacebar.**

n. Below the body text box, click **Add Lookup to Body.**

o. In the **Define Workflow Lookup** dialog box, in the **Field** drop-down list, scroll down, and select **Name.**

p. Click **OK.**

q. Press the **Spacebar,** type *has been approved.* and then click **OK.**

4. Check the workflow for errors.

   a. Click **Check Workflow** to check if the workflow contains any errors.

   b. In the **Microsoft Office SharePoint Designer** message box, click **OK.**

   c. In the **Workflow Designer - Approval Workflow** wizard, click **Finish** to complete the workflow creation.

The following milestones must be performed by the instructor.

5. Test the first step of the approval workflow.

a. Switch to the **GLOBAL\syoung** login account.

b. Launch Internet Explorer.

c. In the Internet Explorer window, in the **Address** bar, click and type ***http://[site name]/HumanResources*** and press **Enter.**

d. If necessary, in the **Connect to** dialog box, type your name and password and click **OK.**

e. In the **HR Document Library** Web Part, click **Upload.**

f. Click **Browse** and then in the **Choose file** dialog box, navigate to the **C:\ 084721Data\Automating Business Process with Workflows** folder and open the **Samantha_Developer.doc** document.

g. Click **OK.**

h. If necessary, scroll down to view the uploaded document.

i. In the **HR Document Library** Web Part, in the **Name** column, place the mouse pointer over the Samantha_Developer link and from the drop-down list, select **Workflows.**

j. On the **Workflows: Samantha_ Developer** page, in the **Start a New Workflow** section, click **Approval Workflow.**

k. On the **Approval Workflow** page, click

Start to manually start the workflow.

l. In the **HR Tasks** Web Part, observe that a new task has been created and assigned to Bob Wheeler.

m. Switch to the **GLOBAL\bwheeler** login account.

n. Choose **Start→E-mail** to launch Microsoft Office Outlook.

o. If necessary, on the **Standard** toolbar, click **Send/Receive** to refresh the **Inbox.**

p. Observe that a new email has arrived specifying that the resume verification task has been assigned to you.

6. Test the second step of the approval workflow.

a. In the **Inbox,** select the new email.

b. In the **Reading Pane,** click the **Samantha_Developer.doc** link and then in the **File Download** dialog box, click **Open.**

c. If necessary, in the **Connect to ogc** dialog box, in the **User name** text box, type **GLOBAL\bwheeler** and in the **Password** text box, type **!Pass1234** and then press **Enter.**

d. In Samantha_Developer.doc, from the Microsoft **Office Button** menu, choose **Server→Check Out.**

e. In the **Edit Offline** message box, click **OK.**

f. View the document and then from the Microsoft **Office Button** menu, choose **Server→Check In.**

g. In the **Check In** dialog box, in the **Version Comments** text box, type **Approved. Please schedule an interview.** and click **OK.**

h. Close Samantha_Developer.doc.

i. Launch Internet Explorer.

j. If necessary, maximize Internet Explorer.

k. In the Internet Explorer window, in the **Address** bar, enter the ***http://[site name]/ HumanResources*** address.

l. In the **HR Tasks** Web Part, in the **Title** column, place the mouse pointer over the new **Resume Verification** task link and from the drop-down list, select **Edit Item.**

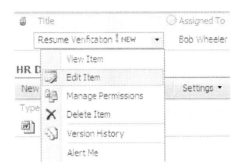

m. On the **Resume Verification** page, click **Complete Task.**

n. Switch to the **GLOBAL\mmiller** login account.

o. Choose **Start→E-mail** to launch Microsoft Office Outlook.

p. In necessary, on the **Standard** toolbar, click **Send/Receive** to refresh the **Inbox.**

q. Observe that there is a new email in the **Inbox** with the specified subject and the lookup text.

r. Close Microsoft Office Outlook.

TOPIC B
Modify a Workflow

You have created a workflow using SharePoint Designer. You can modify the workflow to further include additional steps and decision points without the need to recreate the workflow. In this topic, you will modify a workflow.

When building an application, there will be times when you may need to revisit the design and rework on the application to accommodate the changes. Implementing these changes can be time consuming and may take a lot of effort to fix. But not with SharePoint Designer. SharePoint Designer enables you to make modifications to your existing workflows easily without the need to build the workflow again from scratch.

How to Modify a Workflow

Procedure Reference: Modify a Workflow

To modify a workflow:

1. Open the site containing the workflow you want to modify.
2. Open the Workflow Designer wizard.
   - Choose **File→Open Workflow.**
   - Or, from the **Folder List** task pane, in the website folder, expand the **Workflows** folder and double-click the XOML file.
3. Make the desired changes to the workflow.
   - Add a new step and specify the required actions and conditions.
   - Add a new condition or modify an existing condition in a workflow step.
   - Add a new action or modify an existing action in a workflow step.
   - Add a new Else If conditional branch to a workflow step by clicking the **Add 'Else If' Conditional Branch** link and then adding a new condition and action to it.
4. If necessary, click **Back** and select the desired option.
   - In the **Give a name to this workflow** text box, select the existing name and type the desired name.
   - From the **What SharePoint list should this workflow be attached to** drop-down list, select the necessary list or library item.
   - In the **Select workflow start options for items in Announcements** section, uncheck/check the required options.
5. Click **Check Workflow** to check for any errors in the workflow and if there any errors, rectify the errors.
6. Click **Finish.**
7. Test the workflow.

ACTIVITY 7-2

Modifying a Workflow

Data Files:

Shannon_Developer.doc

Before You Begin:

Switch to your user login and open the Human Resources subsite in SharePoint Designer.

Scenario:

Your HR team has started working with the approval workflow and they want some more enhancements to be made to the approval workflow.

1. The workflow needs to be started once a document is uploaded to the document library.

2. When the functional manager checks the document into the library with the comment "Rejected," the human resource executive should receive an email. Following are the roles involved and their email IDs:

- Susan Young (Human Resource Executive): syoung@ourglobalcompany.com
- Bob Wheeler (Functional Manager): bwheeler@ourglobalcompany.com

What You Do	How You Do It
1. Create an Else If conditional branch for the second step of the workflow.	a. Choose **File→Open Workflow.**
	b. In the **Open Workflow** dialog box, select **Approval Workflow** and click **OK.**
	c. In the **Workflow Designer - Approval Workflow** wizard, in the **Workflow Steps** section, select **Step 2.**
	d. In the **Specify details for 'Step 2'** section, click the **Add 'Else If' Conditional Branch** link.
	e. From the second **Conditions** drop-down list, select **Compare Document Library field.**
	f. Click the **field** link and from the drop-down list, select **Check In Comment.**
	g. Click the **equals** link and from the drop-down list, select **contains.**
	h. Click the **value** link and in the text box, type *Rejected*
	i. From the **Actions** drop-down list, select **Send an Email** and then click the **this message** link.
	j. In the **Define E-mail Message** dialog box, in the **To** text box, type *syoung@ourglobalcompany.com*

 You can enter the email address either by using the address book or by typing the entire email address in the **To** or **CC** text boxes.

What You Do	How You Do It
	k. Next to the **Subject** text box, click **fx.**
	l. In the **Define Workflow Lookup** dialog box, in the **Field** drop-down list, scroll down and select **Name.**
	m. Click **OK.**
	n. Click in the body text box and type *This resume has been rejected.*

o.   Click **OK.**

2.	Set the workflow to start automatically.	a. In the **Workflow Designer - Approval Workflow** wizard, click **Back.**
		b. Uncheck the **Allow this workflow to be manually started from an item** check box.
		c. Check the **Automatically start this workflow item when a new item is created** check box.
3.	Check the workflow for errors.	a. Click **Check Workflow** to check if the workflow contains any errors.
		b. In the **Microsoft Office SharePoint Designer** message box, click **OK.**
		c. In the **Workflow Designer - Approval Workflow** wizard, click **Finish.**

The following milestones must be performed by the instructor.

4. Test the first step of the approval workflow.

   a. Switch to the **GLOBAL\syoung** login account.

   b. Launch the HumanResources subsite in WSS.

   c. In the **HR Document Library** Web Part, click **Upload.**

   d. Click **Browse** and then in the **Choose file** dialog box, select **Shannon_Developer.doc** and click **Open.**

   e. Click **OK** to upload the document.

   f. If necessary, scroll down to view the uploaded document.

   g. Switch to the **GLOBAL\bwheeler** login account.

   h. Launch the HumanResources subsite in WSS.

   i. In the Internet Explorer window, click the **Refresh** button.

   j. On the **default.aspx** page, in the **HR Tasks** Web Part, observe that a new task has been created without the workflow being manually initiated.

   k. Launch Microsoft Office Outlook.

   l. If necessary, on the **Standard** toolbar, click **Send/Receive** to refresh the **Inbox.**

   m. Observe that there is a new email specifying that the resume verification task has been assigned to Bob Wheeler.

5. Test the second step of the approval workflow.	**a.** In the **Reading Pane,** click the **Shannon_ Developer.doc** link and then in the **File Download** dialog box, click **Open.**
	b. In Shannon_Developer.doc, from the **Microsoft Office Button** menu, choose **Server→Check Out.**
	c. In the **Edit Offline** message box, click **OK.**
	d. View the document and then from the **Microsoft Office Button** menu, choose **Server→Check In.**
	e. In the **Check In** dialog box, in the **Version Comments** text box, type *Rejected.* and click **OK.**
	f. Close Shannon_Developer.doc and Microsoft Office Outlook.
	g. In the **HR Tasks** Web Part, in the **Title** column, place the mouse pointer over the new **Resume Verification** task and from the drop-down list, select **Edit Item.**

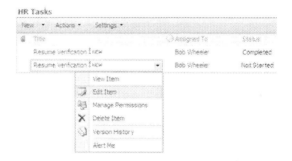

	h. On the **Resume Verification** page, click **Complete Task.**
	i. In the Internet Explorer window, click the **Refresh** button.
	j. Switch to the **GLOBAL\syoung** login account.
	k. Launch Microsoft Office Outlook.
	l. If necessary, on the **Standard** toolbar, click **Send/Receive** to refresh the **Inbox.**
	m. Observe that there is a new email in the **Inbox** with the specified subject and the lookup text.

n. Close Microsoft Office Outlook.

Lesson 7 Follow-up

In this lesson, you created and modified a workflow. SharePoint Designer enables you to integrate business rules and workflow logic into your SharePoint sites without the need to write any code and ensures that your business processes are automated, thereby increasing your workforce efficiency.

1. **What are the common types of business processes that you can automate using SharePoint Designer?**

2. **List some instances when modifying the workflows yields effective results.**

3. **Specify instances when you will create workflows with more than one Else If conditional branches.**

Follow-up

In this course, you developed a subsite using SharePoint Designer. SharePoint Designer enables you to create and customize Microsoft SharePoint sites and build sophisticated application interfaces and workflows on the SharePoint platform.

1. **What according to you are the advantages of creating a subsite using SharePoint Designer?**

2. **What features of SharePoint Designer will you use the most? Are there features you will not use?**

What's Next?

Microsoft® SharePoint® Designer 2007: Level 1 is the first course in a two-part series. The next course is *Microsoft® SharePoint® Designer 2007: Level 2*

Lesson Labs

Due to classroom setup constraints, some labs cannot be keyed in sequence immediately following their associated lesson. Your instructor will tell you whether your labs can be practiced immediately following the lesson or whether they require separate setup from the main lesson content.

Lesson 1 Lab 1

Getting Familiar with SharePoint Designer

Objective:

Familiarize yourself with the SharePoint Designer environment.

Scenario:

You are planning to design a website for your company. But before you begin with the designing process, you want to familiarize yourself with the SharePoint Designer interface and also customize the SharePoint Designer environment to suit your requirements. You also want to find some information from SharePoint Designer Help.

---

1. **Which region of the SharePoint Designer interface displays the web page?**

   a) Quick tag selector

   b) Page view

   c) Tabbed file chooser

   d) Work area

---

2. **Which is the default toolbar in SharePoint Designer?**

   a) Style

   b) Common

   c) Formatting

   d) Tables

---

3. **True or False? You cannot rename the files in the Folder List task pane.**

   __ True

   __ False

---

4. Customize the SharePoint Designer interface by adding or removing a task pane or a toolbar to match your development requirements.

---

5. Find information on the topic of your interest from **SharePoint Designer Help**.

Lesson 2 Lab 1

Creating the Layout of a Subsite

Objective:

Create the layout of a subsite.

Data Files:

background.jpg, banner1.jpg, contactus finance.jpg

Before You Begin:

Switch to your user login.

Scenario:

You are assigned to create a subsite for the Finance team in your organization. You have been given the layout specifications as well as the initial set of images for creating the site.

1. Create a new subsite named **Finance.**

2. Create a new ASPX page.

3. In the **Layout Tables** task pane, select the **Header, Footer, and 3 Columns** layout and then in the layout table, delete the footer section.

4. Using the **Table properties** dialog box, center align the table and set the table width to 1000 pixels.

5. Set the width of the left and middle body sections to 150 and 660 pixels, respectively.

6. Set the **background.JPG** image in the **C:\084721Data\Creating a Subsite\ background.JPG** folder, as the page background and for the second cell below the header section, set white as the background color.

7. Add the **banner1.JPG** image to the header section and set *Our Global Company* as the alternate text.

8. In the third cell below the header section, add the **contactus finance.JPG** image and set *Contact Us* as the alternate text.

9. Set the second cell below the header section as the content region and name it as *Content.*

10. Delete the empty **<form#form1>** tag and the **<p>** tag and save the page as *layout.master.* Save the images in the **images** folder.

Lesson 3 Lab 1

Adding Content to the Web Pages

Objective:

Add content to the web pages.

Data Files:

financialreports.aspx, guidelines.aspx, contactusfinance.aspx, sean.JPG, importantdates.aspx, homepage.doc

Scenario:

The layout of the site is ready. You want to create web pages with the same layout and add relevant content to the pages.

1. Open the **default.aspx** page of the **Finance** subsite and attach it to the **default.master** page.

2. On the **default.aspx** page, in the **PlaceHolderPageDescription (Master)** region, insert a table with one row and two columns.

3. Copy text from the homepage.doc file from the C:\084721Data\Adding Content folder and paste it on the first row of the **default.aspx** page using the **Normal Paragraphs without line breaks** option.

4. Change the color of the text to blue.

5. Insert the **sean.JPG** image from the C:\084721Data\Adding Content folder, in the second column of the **default.aspx** page.

PlaceHolderPageDescription (Custom)

Welcome to the Finance Department of OGC! This site acts as a one-stop location for the employees to get to know the finance policies and guidelines, financial reports of the company, and also submit bills.

6. Remove the black border from the **sean.JPG** image.

7. Import the **financialreports.aspx, guidelines.aspx, importantdates.aspx,** and **contactusfinance.aspx** pages to the **Finance** subsite. Attach the **financialreports.aspx, guidelines.aspx,** and **contactusfinance.aspx** pages to the **layout.master** page.

Lesson 4 Lab 1

Formatting Web Pages Using CSS

Objective:

Format web pages using CSS.

Scenario:

You have finished adding the required web pages to the Finance team subsite of the Our Global Company site. You realize that you are yet to format the text and the other elements on the web pages. Instead of applying formatting to individual pages, you decide to use CSS and apply formatting to all the pages at once.

1. In a new style sheet, create a style for the header (h2) text and para (p) text.

   Style properties for header text:
   - **font-family: Arial**
   - **font-size: 22px**
   - **font-weight: bold**
   - **color: #003399**
   - **left padding: 5px**

   Style properties for para text:
   - **font-family: Arial**
   - **font-size: 12px**
   - **left padding: 5px**

2. Create a new folder called **CSS** and save the external style sheet as **styles.css** in the "CSS" folder.

3. Attach styles.css to layout.master.

4. Save layout.master and update all the linked pages.

5. Open financialreports.aspx.

6. Create class-based styles for blue and gray backgrounds.

    Style properties for `.bluebg` style:
    - **font-family: Arial**
    - **font-size: small**
    - **font-weight: bold**
    - **background-color: #99CCFF**

    Style properties for `.graybg` style:
    - **font-family: Arial**
    - **font-size: 12px**
    - **background-color: #C0C0C0**

7. On the **financialreports.aspx** page, apply the `.bluebg` style to the first row, and the `.graybg` style to the rest of the rows of the table.

Year	Q1	Q2	Q3
2007	$50 million	$70 million	$80.5 million
2006	$51 million	$54 million	$69 million
2005	$37.5 million	$35 million	$36 million
2004	$30.5 million	$28 million	$17 million

8. Move the class-based styles to the styles.css.

9. Save all the pages.

Lesson 5 Lab 1

Linking Pages on a Website

Objective:

Link pages on a website.

Scenario:

The Finance subsite now contains a number of standalone web pages. You want to interlink the web pages, so that the user can navigate the site easily.

1. On the **contactusfinance.aspx** page, add an email hyperlink *finance@ourglobalcompany.com* after the last sentence and save the page.

2. On the **layout.master** page, on the right side image, create a rectangular hotspot around the text "Contact Us". Link it to contactusfinance.aspx, and save the page.

3. On the **guidelines.aspx** page, select the **Late Stay Reimbursement** section heading and add a bookmark with the same name. Select the second line on the page and convert it into a hyperlink targeting the **Late Stay Reimbursement** bookmark.

   Similarly, add a bookmark and a hyperlink for the **Local Conveyance** section. Save the page and test the bookmark.

4. On the **guidelines.aspx** page, below the "Local Conveyance" hyperlink, add an interactive button of your choice and name it as **Important Dates.**

   ## Policies and Guidelines

   Late Stay Reimbursement

   Local Conveyance

   Important Dates

5. Use the **Open Browser Window** behavior to link the interactive button to the **importantdates.aspx** page. Set the window name of the new browser as *OGC* and the window width to 450 pixels and the window height to 220 pixels. Save and preview the pages.

Lesson 6 Lab 1

Working with SharePoint Components

Objective:

Work with SharePoint components.

Scenario:

In order to share information among the team members of the Finance department, you want to have a Tasks list and a Document Library on the home page of the subsite. You also want to change the title of the list and the library item to match that of the subsite. To further enhance the functionality, you plan to add a navigation structure for the subsite that includes a link bar and a **Quick Launch** bar. You also plan to add a link to the **Top Link** bar of the main site that points to the Finance subsite.

1. Add a **Tasks** list and a **Document Library** to the Finance subsite. Name them as *Finance Tasks* and *Invoice Library* respectively.

2. Insert a Web Part zone in the **PlaceHolderMain(Custom)** content region of the **default.aspx** page of the **Finance** subsite.

3. Place the **Finance Tasks** and the **Invoice Library** Web Part inside the Web Part zone on the **default.aspx** page of the **Finance** subsite.

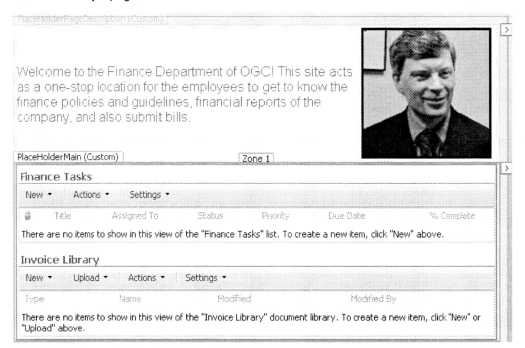

4. Add the **Check In Comment** field to the **Invoice Library** Web Part and save the page.

5. Add a link bar on the **layout.master** page of the **Finance** subsite with links pointing to the organization's main site and to the home page of the Finance subsite. Name the links as OGC Home and OGC Finance respectively. Choose a desired style for the link bar. Save the **layout.master** page.

6. Add links for the **financialreports.aspx, guidelines.aspx,** and **contactusfinance.aspx** pages in the **Quick Launch** bar of the **Finance** subsite. Name the links as Financial Reports, Guidelines, and Contact Us.

7. Add a link for the Finance subsite to the **Top Link** bar of the OGC site and name it as Finance.

8. Preview the pages of the subsite and test the links added to the **Link** bar, **Quick Launch** bar, and the **Top Link** bar.

Lesson 7 Lab 1

Creating a Workflow

Objective:

Create a workflow.

Data Files:

Invoice.doc

Before You Begin:

As this activity involves three roles, it requires a user and email IDs for each role. Ensure that Microsoft Office Outlook has been configured for all the three users.

Scenario:

The development of the Finance subsite is complete. You now want to automate the bill approval process. The process is as follows:

1. When the employee posts the invoice to the document library, a task needs to be assigned for the employee's functional manager to review the invoice.

2. The functional manager, on viewing the task, checks out the invoice, reviews it, and places the appropriate comment while checking it back into the library. The functional manager also completes the task assigned.

3. Once the invoice is checked back into the library with the comment "Approved," the finance executive should receive an email permitting the executive to process the bill.

4. If the invoice is checked into the library with the comment "Rejected," the employee should receive an email asking the employee to make the necessary changes.

---

1. Open the Workflow Designer wizard.

---

2. Set **Invoice Approval** as the workflow name. Link it to the Invoice Library and make the workflow to be initiated automatically whenever a new item is created.

---

3. On the specify details page, select the **Compare Invoice Library field** condition and set it to perform an action if the name of the document contains the word "Invoice".

---

4. Set the workflow to assign a task called **Invoice Verification** to the manager once the document has been uploaded.

---

5. Create a new step and set the workflow to send an email to the finance assistant if the manager's checkin comment specifies that the document has been approved.

---

6. Create an Else If conditional branch to send an email back to the employee if the document has been rejected by the manager.

7. Check the workflow for errors and finish the workflow.

8. Test the workflow.

Solutions

Lesson 1

Activity 1-1

2. **Which option in the editing window allows you to navigate among multiple web pages?**

   a) The work area

   b) Page views

   ✓ c) The tabbed file chooser

   d) The quick tag selector bar

4. **Which view enables you to see the changes happening on the web page as you work on its code?**

   a) The Code view

   b) The Design view

   ✓ c) The Split view

   d) The page view

Lesson 1 Follow-up

Lesson 1 Lab 1

1. **Which region of the SharePoint Designer interface displays the web page?**

   a) Quick tag selector

   b) Page view

   c) Tabbed file chooser

   ✓ d) Work area

2. **Which is the default toolbar in SharePoint Designer?**

   a) Style

   ✓ b) Common

   c) Formatting

   d) Tables

3. **True or False? You cannot rename the files in the Folder List task pane.**

   ___ True

   ✓ False

Lesson 4

Activity 4-1

1. **Which one of these is not a style sheet?**

   ✓ a) Class

   b) Inline

   c) External

   d) Internal

2. **True or False? An element-based style applies the style for every instance of a particular element.**

   ✓ True

   ___ False

3. **Which of these options are style types?**

   ✓ a) Class

   b) External

   ✓ c) Element

   ✓ d) ID

4. **What defines the syntax of a style?**

   a) CSS

   b) Styles

   c) Selectors

   ✓ d) Rules

5. **What are the constituents of a declaration?**

   a) Selectors

   ✓ b) Value

   c) Rules

   ✓ d) Property

Glossary

action

A task performed when triggered by an event.

Apply Styles task pane

A task pane that provides you with options to create a new style, attach an external style sheet, and list all the styles available in different categories.

behavior

A combination of an event and a resulting action. It helps you to add interactivity to the websites you create.

bookmark link

A hyperlink that connects to a specific target location either within the same page or on a different page.

bookmark

A label given to a specific section of a web page.

condition

A condition, when returns true, triggers an action.

content region

A region defined in a master page that facilitates the addition of content that changes with each page.

context menu

A menu that appears when you right-click elements such as toolbars and task panes.

CSS Properties task pane

A context-sensitive task pane that enables you to add and modify the CSS properties of the selected element.

CSS rule

A rule that defines the syntax of a style.

CSS

(Cascading Style Sheet) A style language that can control the appearance of documents written in HTML, XML or XHTML languages.

declaration

A part of style rule that contains the list of properties and values.

event

A parameter that triggers an action.

external style sheet

A style sheet in which styles are defined on a separate page.

Formatting toolbar

A toolbar that contains options to change the font type, size, and other basic text properties.

hotspot

A hyperlink that is defined for a part of an image.

hyperlink state

Status of a hyperlink defined by user activity.

hyperlink
A text or image link on a web page that connects to another section of the same page or another web page.

Import dialog box
A dialog box that allows you to add files and even entire folders to the website folder.

inline style sheet
A style sheet that affects the HTML element (tag) that they are directly applied to.

interactive button
A button with a link functionality that not only changes its appearance based on the users' mouse movement over the button, but also links to another page.

internal style sheet
A style sheet, also called embedded style sheet, controls the formatting for the web page on which they are embedded.

Layout Tables task pane
Enables you to design the layout of a web page.

layout
A framework that helps you to control the placement of elements on a web page.

link bar
A collection of hyperlinks arranged vertically or horizontally on the web page and are used to provide a navigation system for a site.

Manage Styles task pane
A powerful CSS tool used to manage your styles.

master page
An ASP.NET page that enables you to automatically display the standard elements of a website on all pages.

Navigation view
An application pane that displays a graphical and hierarchical view of the site structure.

Pictures toolbar
A toolbar that contains several options that enable you to modify an image in a file.

Quick Launch bar
A list of links that is displayed on the left side of a page in a SharePoint site.

safety net feature
A feature in SharePoint Designer that allows you to revert to the default master page/ stylesheet scheme after being customized.

selector
A keyword that selects the element you want to style.

SharePoint Designer Help
A feature in SharePoint Designer that acts as a central location where you can learn how to work with the software, solve problems, and obtain product support information.

SharePoint document library
A content structure in a SharePoint site that contains files.

SharePoint list
A content structure in a SharePoint site that contains a group of similar items.

site collection
A collection of websites on a web server.

style
A set of formatting options, which are defined in a CSS.

subsite
A website that is stored inside a top-level site.

Tag Properties task pane
A context-sensitive task pane that displays all the properties of a selected tag.

Top Link bar
A collection of links that appear as tabs at the top of the home page in a SharePoint site.

top-level site
The main site where the administrator settings for a site collection are changed.

Web Part zone
A modular unit in a SharePoint site that contains Web Parts.

Web Part

The basic design element of a SharePoint site that contains information.

workflow

Comprises a series of tasks performed in succession to produce a final outcome.

Index